Young Hollywood Actors

Young Hollywood Actors

How They Got Started, How They Keep Going:
Stories & Advice from Your Favorite Performers

The Hometown to Hollywood Interviews
Volume I

Bonnie J. Wallace

Hollywood
Parents
Press

Published in the United States by Hollywood Parents Press.

ISBN 978-0-9863511-2-9
ISBN 978-0-9863511-3-6
1. Performing Arts. 2. Acting and Auditioning.

Library of Congress Control Number: 2018913788
Hollywood Parents Press: Los Angeles, California

www.bonniejwallace.com

While the author has made every effort to provide accurate Internet addresses and resource information at the time of publication, neither the publisher nor the author assumes any responsibility for errors or for changes that occur after publication. In addition, publisher does not have any control over and does not assume any responsibility for author or third-party websites or their content.

For Claire, Chloe, and Bobby
You fill my life with love and inspiration

And

For all the dreamers
And those who support them

Individual Cover Photo Credits

Contents

Gratitude

THIS BOOK WOULD not exist without the incredible generosity of the twelve young actors who took time out of their busy lives to speak so honestly with me for the *Hometown to Hollywood* podcast and then gave me permission to share their words in this book. Their success is a testament to their passion, creativity, and hard work. A huge thank you to:

Luke Benward
Cameron Boyce
Joey Bragg
Dove Cameron
Garrett Clayton
Brenna D'Amico
Thomas Doherty
Jessica Marie Garcia
Sarah Jeffery
Victoria Moroles
Dylan Playfair
Booboo Stewart

Special thanks to Roberta Raye, Kate Carruthers, Anne Wilkinson Ellis, Lisa Skelly, Catherine Kennedy, Debra Gilmore, Lorene Harriman, Cheryl Schneiderhan, Dana Wells Boyd, Tay Brumit, Bob Wallace, June Wallace, Kristin Wolfram, Graehm Wallace, Sandy Wallace, Sarah Wallace, Pamela Fisher, Harry Abrams, Domina Holbeck, Fatmata Kamara, Jennifer Davisson, Phillip Watson, Patti Felker, Corey Barash, Scott Felcher, Alex Schack, Betsy Sullenger, Andy Fickman, John Beck, Ron Hart, Kenny Ortega, Gary Marsh, Steve Vincent, Suzanne Goddard-Smyth, and Dinah Manoff.

Very special thanks to Robert Bellospirito. Most of all, my greatest love and deepest gratitude to my two daughters, Claire Hosterman and Dove Cameron (Chloe). My days, and this book, are dedicated to you.

Introduction

OVER EIGHT YEARS ago, my youngest daughter, Dove, and I packed up everything we owned and drove from Bainbridge Island to Los Angeles to give her a chance at her dream.

When we landed in LA, I was stunned by how little effective, trustworthy help there was for parents of young actors trying to navigate Hollywood. There was plenty of hype, but helping Dove get her start in the entertainment industry felt overwhelming, challenging, and frustrating.

When Dove reached a clear level of success, I knew I wanted to give back by helping other families. I began a blog; wrote *The Hollywood Parents Guide;* started the *Hometown to Hollywood* podcast; and began consulting, speaking, and teaching workshops.

My mission is to educate and inspire. Education helps you make the best decisions for *you.* Inspiration helps you persevere when the going gets tough—as it can for everyone.

This book shares that mission and is the first in a series based on the *Hometown to Hollywood* interviews. I'm excited to bring the thoughtful, honest, and raw words of twelve extraordinary young artists to you in these pages.

If you enjoy this book, I encourage you to subscribe to the podcast. You can find it on iTunes, or on my website: https://bonniejwallace.com. The website's player works on all major platforms, not just Apple, and you'll get the show notes there. As of this writing, there are over eighty episodes published, with more to come.

It's my hope that the authentic and intimate stories shared in this book will both shed light on what it really takes to become a successful young actor and inspire you to follow your own dreams, whatever they may be.

Bonnie

BONUS:
You can download the unpublished *bonus chapters* from this book at https://bonniejwallace.com/bonus-chapters/! These incredible chapters couldn't be included in the final manuscript due to length issues. Find out what it was like for these young actors to land in Hollywood, who inspires them, what they would do if they weren't actors, how they stay focused on their dreams, and *more*!

1

When Did You Know You Wanted to Be an Actor?

WHEN DO YOU know you've discovered your life's path?

Some people know what they want to do before they even have the words for it. As Dove Cameron said, "I don't know, it's like—do you remember when your first word was? I was just kind of always speaking. I was just kind of always wanting to be an actor."

Other people discover their true calling in the course of pursuing something else. Dylan Playfair was focused on hockey until he was nineteen and realized that he wasn't going to make it professionally as a hockey player. Only then did he begin to think about pursuing acting...and his hockey background actually helped him find an agent and some of his first roles.

Brenna D'Amico and Thomas Doherty discovered their love of acting through taking classes when they were young. Victoria Moroles, Cameron Boyce, and Sarah Jeffery discovered performing through dance. Luke Benward and Booboo Stewart had parents in the entertainment industry, which gave them early exposure and opportunities. Jessica Marie Garcia fell in love with movies, and Joey Bragg fell in love with stand-up comedy. Garrett Clayton began his career in commercial modeling and then pursued musical theater before moving into film and TV.

For every one of these young stars, the path was different, but a few things were shared: a belief in themselves, perseverance, and strong parental support.

Two of those three things are available to anyone. And while parental support is helpful at any age, once you are eighteen, you can find a way to pursue your path on your own if necessary.

Dove Cameron

Dove: I don't know, it's like—do you remember what your first word was? I was just kind of always speaking. I was just kind of always wanting to be an actor. There was definitely a time where I had a bigger melting pot of career options, as you know, I thought maybe I want to do fashion design. There was even a time where I thought I might want to be a lawyer. When you're younger, the possibilities of doing all three are totally viable. I was going to be a fashion designer lawyer, actor on the side (laughs).

There was a time when, honestly, I went through a bit of a...childhood to teen-hood depression. Which I think a lot of creative, intelligent kids go through because it's just really difficult to grapple with all of your feelings plus all of the new lessons, plus all of the hormones and the changing...that moodiness, that can dip into depression sometimes, and I've seen it a lot in young kids.

I would just stay up all night watching films, and that was the only thing that interested me. I would only watch films, or television, and a lot of my cultural references and life lessons that I would talk to you about, you'd say, "Where'd you learn that?" And I'd be like "Oh, this show" or "Oh, that movie," and I just started to notice that that was literally the only thing that I cared about.

That was what took up 100 percent of my brain, and that was what I wanted to take up 100 percent of my life. I don't think it was ever a decision. It was just...I just knew that. Then obviously when I—it's so funny, I'm talking to a bunch of strangers by talking to my mom...When I convinced you to move to LA at fourteen, I don't really remember that time with much clarity, but I remember that I knew that that's what I wanted to do. I'd known that for a long time, you know? I don't know, I don't think there was ever a time when I had decided to do it. It was just something I always was going to do.

Bonnie: I know that when you were really young, you were begging me to get you into the local theater we had.

Dove: Right, like seven, and I don't know why.

Bonnie: I also remember resisting it for as long as I could.

Dove: Well, that's because you're into theater, and you knew what it was like. Theater can sometimes be a bit dangerous. Not really, but a lot of thespians can be pretty intense. Yeah, I think I probably wanted to get into the theater because you and Claire were doing it, and it was either that I wanted to be like you or I wanted to compete with you. I don't know; I was always out to prove myself, in terms of, I can run with the adults, I can run with the best of them, I am an unstoppable force of nature. I just needed to be doing what the adults were doing.

Then what got me into film and television, I swear, it was just that I had my own laptop and I had access to all those things. Watching everything. I used to just go on IMDb and become obsessed with an actor or an actress and watch everything that they did.

Brenna D'Amico

Brenna: I was really shy when I was younger, so it was when my friend started doing musical theater when I was eight, and my mom kind of talked me into doing it with her. I was so shy. We had to go to different parks until we could find nobody there. It was crazy.

I would go to the park, but I was so shy that if we'd find kids there, we'd have to leave, but then when my friend did a stage play for musical theater, I said, "Okay, Mom, I'm gonna do it," and I fell in love with it. I fell in love. I absolutely fell in love, and that's when I knew I was hooked.

Bonnie: Isn't that interesting? I think there's a lot of people out there who think that actors can't be shy people, but in my experience, a lot of actors are actually very shy people.

Brenna: Yeah, I know, and that's what kind of broke me out of my shell and let me experience new things because from that day forward, that's when I started gradually getting more outgoing, and I'm really grateful that that happened for me.

Bonnie: It gave you courage.

Brenna: Yeah, it did give me so much courage and bravery, and when I would perform on that stage, I knew that's what

I wanted to do for the rest of my life, so that's what really inspired me.

Bonnie: That just gave me chills. You were eight?

Brenna: I was eight, and I did musical theater up until I was twelve, and that's when I found my manager in Chicago.

Booboo Stewart

Booboo: I've grown up on set my whole life, living in LA, my father being in the business. I just always wanted to be there and hang out. When I saw Heath Ledger play the Joker in *The Dark Knight*, his performance made me think back to the times when I was really young, and I saw skateboarders, and I thought, "That's so cool. I want to be a skateboarder." When I saw that, I thought, "That's amazing. I want to be an actor." Yeah, I was fifteen.

Bonnie: He inspired you?

Booboo: Immensely. Crazy. Yeah, because I've grown up around it and I always had done things on sets. Helping my dad with stunts. I did music. Just because you're living in LA, you're exposed to so many different kinds of things. That performance made me want to be an actor.

Garrett Clayton

Garrett: I'm trying to think. It was weird. It was like a buildup of realizing this is the thing I'm going to do. I started in commercial modeling when I was thirteen in Chicago and Detroit. My mom's friend was currently modeling, and my mom had done it for a minute when she was younger. They knew an agent that I went to who knew an agent in Chicago.

I don't know if it's a typical story, but the parent helps the kid, which you fully understand. It was never pushed on me. It was always something I really wanted. I said, "I want to try this," and she said, "Okay, if you get your grades up and you work hard, then I'll let you try it. I'll work the hours, and I'll get the money so we can...I'll give you a really fair shot at this." She goes, "But one thing, nothing will happen for ten years."

It was the first thing she said to me. She goes, "You're gonna work really hard, and it's gonna be really long, and you're probably not going to get a lot of things to start, and it will take ten years before it even starts."

She says, "Are you okay with that?" As a kid, I was, "Oh, okay, yeah. Sure, that's fine." Now, looking back...*Teen Beach Movie* came out when I was twenty-two, twenty-three. That was when it kind of clicked, "Oh, it just started." I got my first movie, on accident, when I was fifteen, and I started in community theater doing these random, weird shows. My first play was *Charlotte's Web*, and I didn't know any lines, and I kind of treated it like *Whose Line Is It Anyway?* Because I was such a big fan of the show, I thought I could get away with it.

I guess when you're an uninhibited kid and everybody else is following the script and you are treating it like *Whose Line Is It Anyway?* it is funny for people, but it wasn't appropriate. I thought it was fun, but I quit acting when I was in high school because I wanted to try the swim team. I played seven or eight sports growing up.

Because the rule was, if you don't like something, you have to try something else.

Which I'm happy for now, especially as an actor who has to do a bunch of different things, you know.

Bonnie: Yes, you have access to a lot of skills now.

Garrett: Everything from boxing, horseback riding, football, karate, soccer, swim team, you name it. I think swimming was the last real sport, team sport, I ever played for a period of time. I didn't get as much as I wanted to out of it, and I realized how much I loved acting. So I crawled back to the drama club, and the director begrudgingly took me back. Because when I first was doing it, I was flighty and didn't show up to rehearsals as much.

I found out when they were doing *Peter Pan*. I really wanted to be Peter. They were doing set building during the summer for *Fame*. I asked, "Can I have a shot at Peter Pan?" The director goes, "You're going to have to work really hard, because I doubt you're going to get it." She goes, "You're not dedicated. You haven't shown any reason why we should have faith in you having this part, but if you can find some magical way to prove to me that you can handle it, then, yeah, I'll give you a shot." I said, "Okay, what steps can I take?" She goes, "We're doing *Fame*. Audition for that, and show your dedication. Then I'll see if you can audition."

So, I did *Fame*, and I was fully committed. Yeah, I think it was in *Peter Pan* that I realized, I guess. I showed up to the audition. I made an entire costume. I had blocking. I went over to my aunt's house, who helped me create blocking for it. So, in my head there was the two beds here and the window was over there. I went full force with this, and it was great. I got the part the same day because I worked my butt off.

Bonnie: Well, and you had good mentoring. I mean, you had a mom who said, "Yes, I will support you in this, and I'll do my part, but you have to do your part and you have to have a certain set of expectations that are realistic." Then you had that director who told you, "Prove it."

Garrett: Yeah. She said, "Why do you want it? You have to earn it." It was Dove who said it to me, because we were talking about work and our paths when we first started working on *Hairspray* together. She stopped me and said, "You know, no one could ever tell you that you didn't work hard for every single thing you got. Every single thing."

Because we had talked about everything at that point. Yeah, nobody just called and said, "Does he want this thing?" It was always, "He can audition for it."

Bonnie: Yes. And you had to work for it, and you had to earn it, and that's a beautiful place to be. Because that's something you can really stand on. That's a very firm thing to be grounded in, as a human, never mind as an actor.

So there you were, you're in high school. You get *Peter Pan*; then what? You were living in Detroit, right?

Garrett: I grew up all over Detroit metro. I lived in five states before I was four. My parents split up, and then my dad lived in Redford off Five Mile and Inkster, and my mom lived in Canton off of Shelly and Ford Rd. It's just completely different communities of people. Not to say any are better or worse. It's just different.

So, I finished *Peter Pan*. It's so crazy just thinking back to all these things. I never take the time to think about it. It's kind of fun.

I realized how much I loved it, and then we were going to do *Beauty and the Beast* and *Barefoot in the Park*. Luckily, the director, she really loves doing one classic thing and then one modern thing every year.

So, we'd gotten to do dramas and...I've found a love for comedy because of *Barefoot in the Park*, getting to be Paul. Really realizing, believing in the moments...it's not playing the comedy. The comedy comes from the reality.

So that was a big awakening in my acting as well. I learned how to sing for *Beauty and the Beast*. I originally was going to get into musical theater, and I got into a program at Oakland University, and I went there for a year.

Through this whole time, I'd been traveling on Greyhounds back and forth with my mom to go to Chicago. I'd done some random guest spots. I went to a casting call for *Days of Our Lives* that I booked, and I got to do this really cool movie with Ed Harris and Jennifer Connelly. I mean, I got to do really cool, random, small things through this whole process...model for Guess and do ads that were international. So I got to get a little small taste of things because of the film industry coming to Michigan and going through high school, bouncing back and forth with taking my homework on the Greyhounds and working, getting back on it, coming back home, next day go back to school.

Dylan Playfair

Dylan: I first, if you couldn't guess, wanted to be a hockey player. I was playing hockey from the time I was two years old. My parents had us out on skates, and I was playing organized hockey right up until I was nineteen. I was playing Junior A hockey. I'd moved away from home at seventeen to play Junior B. It was my everything. I loved it. It was a sport that I saw myself doing for the rest of my life.

It was around the summer of 2011, going into my nineteen-year-old season that I started watching *Friday Night Lights* with Taylor Kitsch, who was another guy who played in the same league. I had a fun season, but I had a really hard season. I had a couple concussions, I didn't score many goals. I was really seeing the writing on the wall that maybe if I want to keep doing hockey, I'm going to have to transition out of being a player, because I wasn't going to make the NHL. In my head, at that time, I put that roadblock in front of me.

There was an opportunity through another kid on the team. His dad had, in a passing conversation, said, "You know, Vancouver's got a booming film industry." And it was something always at the back of my head. I thought, "You know, if I'm going to do it, I should do it now because I'm going to put another two years into hockey and then go for four years in university, and I can take those six years and let's roll the dice on an acting career." I loaded up my Chrysler Sebring, drove to Vancouver, and lived in Silvan Harper's parents' house and worked as a PA scout.

So I was out, looking for locations with the location guys and then working, watching generators and bagging garbage cans, just asking everyone on set how they got into it, and then I got the opportunity to play pick-up hockey with an actor who was a day player. I was just smitten. I said, "You make your living acting? How do you do that, man? I want to do that, but I don't know how." So I just asked a lot of people, and people were really, really helpful with shedding light on their journeys and introducing me to people who would help a little bit further.

I ended up going to an acting school, a Vancouver acting school, studied there for a couple months, went and took a lot of classes with Matthew Harrison and various casting directors. Through that B league team that I was playing hockey on, I met Jerry Kissel, who introduced me to his former agent who signed me. Fast-forward five years, and we're on a TV show together. That's a very condensed, long form of how and when I became an actor.

Bonnie: That is so cool. So, you didn't even start until you were nineteen?

Dylan: Did not set foot on a film set. I had done a little bit of high school theater, but at that time, again, I was playing hockey...I played *Hamlet* in a school play, which was probably the most stressful play that I've ever done because of my schedule. I was there for about a third of the rehearsals, but I really fell in love with it. I fell in love with the energy of being on stage, and I told them, "If you do give me an opportunity to play this guy, I'll make sure I fit in with a third of the rehearsal time." And he said, "Okay, you can play the role, but you're going to have to work really hard to make it work." And we did. And I never forgot that feeling in the eleventh grade of being on that stage, and I wanted it again, and it's become my life now.

Bonnie: And you made it happen. I love that you started out as a PA (production assistant) and just doing whatever needed to be done, bagging garbage, scouting locations.

Dylan: I just had no idea how else how to do it, and that to me was the first step. A lot of people said, "You should get behind the camera or you should get in front of the camera. Whatever you do, you need to get off of this particular department." I wouldn't have known that had I not been in that department. For me, anything was better than nothing. Just being around the industry was for me enough to be in film. I knew that feeling was so nice that acting would be so much more rewarding, and it shed some light on a couple of different paths and opportunities. The ones that I've chosen have worked out.

Jessica Marie Garcia

Jessica: I don't believe there's anything else I really wanted to be in life. I remember watching *Funny Girl* when I was super young. I think I was eight. I saw Barbara Streisand, and she was so funny and so different and had a voice that was unbelievable. I don't have that part, but her acting was just unreal, and she had so much power, and I thought, "I want to do this. How do I do this?"

As soon as I told my mom, she just gave me so many movies to watch. I grew up watching Elizabeth Taylor and Bette Davis and just aspiring to be them. There was nothing else I wanted to do. I wanted to be them. I wanted to hold everyone's attention like they did.

Bonnie: Part of your mom's response was to give you a bunch of quality movies to watch?

Jessica: Oh yeah. She was very much, "If you're going to do this, I want you to be the best. She loved movies. My mom was a dancer. She doesn't dance now other than in our living room. She loved film and…if I wanted to pursue that, then she wanted me to watch the best of it.

Bonnie: That's so cool. You were around eight, and you fell in love with these great actors.

Jessica: I'm an only child. Being an only child, I feel like you put on shows on your own for your stuffed animals and things. I was always performing, I would say. I think it was instilled in me at birth.

Bonnie: Did she sign you up for acting classes?

Jessica: No. Funny enough, that's what's so interesting about my mom. She was so hands-on at that moment. You need to watch this, you need to do this—but she never said for me to do anything. I took my own lead, and she just always supported me. She was always the one that I ran to. I was like, "Oh, I'm doing this," but she never was the one signing me up for anything.

I tried out for my first play. It was *Midsummer Night's Dream*. I was in sixth grade. That was my first audition experience. It was in a classroom, and I had the paper in front of my face. It was horrible, and I just screamed everything because I was so nervous. I was a fairy in one of them. "Mustard Seed," that was my name. I had two lines. It was great. I think they were one word. Then from there, I ended up being Phoebe, and I also liked it, and it grew from there. She was always my supporter, but she never had me do anything.

Bonnie: Support is huge.

Jessica: The support is ridiculous. She blindly moved out here for me, but she never knew. I remember a time I told my mom, "I got a callback." She's like, "Oh, that's great," and then I told her, "Mom, I'm going to network callbacks." "Didn't you just do that?"

No, it's really different. This is a much bigger deal, so she just gets really excited, but she has no idea how the business works, none whatsoever.

I love it that way actually.

Joey Bragg

Joey: I don't know if I still know whether I want to be an actor or not. I always knew that I didn't want to do something like an office job or nine to five. I just knew that I wanted to do something different. Unconventional. But I didn't really know what it was.

When I was in elementary school, we had a yo-yo guy come to our school that did yo-yo tricks. He said, "I went to Paris," and he made an Eiffel Tower, and I thought, "That. That is what I want to be. I want to be the yo-yo guy that goes to children and entertains them with tricks." And then I got pretty good at a yo-yo, which everybody that loves *Liv and Maddie* has probably seen.

And then I just kinda threw that to the wind, and certain things came up like that. I was a drummer for a while. I solved a Rubik's cube really fast, but nothing really stuck, and then I saw the movie *Funny People* by Judd Apatow, and I was like, "I get it. I get how stand-up comedy works. I've always wanted to be the funny guy in the room." So I thought, "Now I want to understand how you write jokes," and I started writing a lot of jokes and not performing them. I just had a book that was full of different premises and things when I was twelve, and then my brother found the book and said, "Hey, man, did you write this? These are really funny." And that was the only nice thing he's ever said to me.

And so after that, I went up on stage at a coffeehouse in San Jose for an open mic.

Bonnie: How old were you?

Joey: Fresh turned thirteen.

Bonnie: That's amazing.

Joey: Yeah. But it isn't…I mean my dad told me when I was a lit-
            tle kid that nobody can tell the difference between fake

confidence and real confidence, and so once I learned that, I would go around school thinking I was the most confident guy in school, and then everybody would be like, "He's so confident." You ever seen the movie *Fast Times at Ridgemont High*?

Mike Damone, the guy that sells tickets and had that scene with a girl...I watched that movie when I was a little kid thinking, "That's the guy I wanna be. I want that demeanor. I want everyone to think I'm too cool for school." And so...once you fake confidence enough, and people start believing it, then you start believing in the confidence that was originally feigned. I think I was just too full of myself to not expect that people would want to hear what I have to say.

Bonnie: So you just assumed that it would go well?

Joey: Not really. I didn't assume it would go well. I just assumed that it would make me feel good. When I first went up on stage, it was the weirdest thing 'cause I was at a coffeehouse in San Jose, right after this reggae band that set up, and then a guy was doing slam poetry, and I went up, and my first joke was about how badly I wanted to live in New York but how afraid I would be every time you heard that *Law and Order*, "Dun, dun," because you know somewhere in New York, someone was brutally murdered.

So that was my first joke, and it was such an out-of-body experience to have this audience laughing. I remember feeling like it felt like I was looking up from myself, from above. Then I got a good response, and once you get that first good show, I couldn't stop. I was doing it every night.

Bonnie: You had a lot of real comedy clubs on your résumé when you were sixteen, and we met for the *Bits and Pieces* pilot.

Joey: Oh yeah. 'Cause pretty much, in San Francisco, there's four or five comedy clubs. Some of them more prestigious like Cobb's Comedy Club, and there are ones that are ones I started out like Tommy T's in Pleasanton. Once you get to doing that, and you meet people, and you get a good five minutes or fifteen minutes down, and then more people start inviting you…stand-up is kinda like a car going down a hill that the further you go, the faster it starts to go, and there's nothing really to stop it unless you just stop it. You just get better and better and better, no matter who it is. No stand-ups started really good. Every stand-up starts, and then you find your voice, and once you find your voice, then the ball really starts to roll, and so I think I found my voice pretty early. I mean, earlier than most. It takes some people years. I don't know if that's because I was young or because I was just full of myself.

Bonnie: Or maybe you have a gift. I mean you are a very funny guy.

Joey: It's the thing I was always able to rely on. I wasn't handsome or nice or anything, but I could always make people laugh. I could always brush off any emotion I had with humor, and so it's just something I relied on and then was able to make a living out of it.

Luke Benward

Luke: Growing up, my parents always gave me a choice, always, and they made sure to verbalize with me and make sure that I was choosing to do this, because growing up, I had to sacrifice things as anyone will. You have to sacrifice. I played football, I wanted to play basketball, I wanted to run track. I wasn't able to do that because I would audition during the off season.

I had to change schools my junior year, which was a big sacrifice for me. I had gone to school with the same kids from kindergarten to sophomore year of high school. I had to change, and that was kind of a big step for me, but I think it was important because, to answer your question, around that time was when I felt, "All right, I think I'm ready to take this seriously."

I had done a pilot for Disney...I have a strong love for film and movies and that's just what I had always done growing up, and so I didn't really want to get locked into a pilot unless it was something I was really passionate about. And I ended up doing one for them called *Madison High*, which was really cool. They were basically trying to do *High School Musical* as a TV show.

I was fully expecting that to go, fully accepting the move, the inevitable move to California, so I was kind of already putting myself in that place of, "All right, this is going to be my life now. I'm going to live there." That pilot ended up not going forward, so we stayed in Tennessee, but I had already un-enrolled from my high school, which means I couldn't go there again because we were out of zone. I went to a new high school and continued auditioning, and then Disney came back to me with another pilot.

I told them, "I don't know." And Gary Marsh (the president of Disney Channel) pitched it to me and told me about it and convinced me. I did that, and that was another one where I thought, "All right, let's go. We're going to move." Knowing.

Bonnie: You guys have been living in Tennessee all this time?

Luke: That whole time, yeah. This other pilot comes around, and we've learned from our mistakes. My parents said, "All right, we accept; let's do it. We're going to make it, and whether it goes or not, we're going to move. We're just going to go to LA. Luke, is that what you want?" And I said, "Yes. I'm already away from my friends, I'm not playing football, I'm ready to take it seriously. Let's just go out there."

We moved right in between junior and senior year. I was seventeen.

Bonnie: And at that point that you had so much experience. When I look at your résumé, when I look at your IMDb sheets, it's just shocking to me how much work you had done before you were seventeen, while you were still living in Tennessee. That's amazing.

At that point you probably knew what you were talking about when you said, "I choose this."

Luke: Yeah, totally. I knew that I loved it growing up. I mean, I loved a lot of things growing up, you know. I loved playing outside, but you can't play outside for a living.

Unless you're really good at a sport. I loved football, I loved singing. My parents were amazing in that they gave me a chance to really explore everything that I loved, and they saw that I was good at it. I had a natural gifting. I tried music. I toured, and it was cool. I really enjoyed it, and I had some amazing experiences, but it wasn't the same. I didn't have that feeling, the same kind of feeling of when I'm on set.

When I stopped playing football, and I really didn't miss it that much, and I got away from my friends and that kind of stuff, I guess I just realized that there was a passion that I didn't have for other things that was continuing to push me to act. There was something telling me that that was what I should be doing.

Bonnie: I love that. I think that's a wonderful way to express that because in my experience just because you're really good at something doesn't mean that that's what you should be doing.

A lot of us are really good at more than one thing, but it doesn't mean that it fills our heart or that it makes sense with the rest of our lives and the rest of our gifts to go for it and make a living at it. I think it's really critical that you have a moment like you did and say, "Yes, this is it. Other things I love and I'm good at it but not as much."

Sarah Jeffery

Sarah: I did my first project when I was about fourteen, and it was just a little pilot presentation for Cartoon Network, and I had two days on it. I got the acting bug, for sure. I wanted to keep doing it. There was sort of a lull. I was auditioning, and nothing was really sticking. I got a little bit discouraged, but I thought, "I'm going to stick with this and see what comes out of it." I auditioned for *Rogue*, and I didn't really think anything of it. I hadn't heard for a while, but I was very passionate about the project because the lead actor is one of my favorite actresses.

We got a call when I was in Las Vegas for a dance competition. They asked, "Can you please come back and read again?" It had been months. I told them, "I'm sorry, I'm just about to go on stage. I can't." We thought, "Dang, I guess that's not going to work out." On the drive home, they called me, "You got the part." It was crazy. I auditioned once, and then months later, it turned out to be my part, which was amazing, and that's definitely when I knew this was what I wanted to do. It was a very emotional show, a lot of hard work, but so rewarding and very eye opening, and I had some great mentors on the show.

Bonnie: You're fourteen when this happens?

Sarah: Yes. I think I turned fifteen when *Rogue* happened. I had done that little Cartoon Network project when I was about fourteen. A year had passed, and nothing had stuck, and I figured, "We'll stick with it." My dad is an actor, and he told me, "I think you've got a lot of potential, so I think you should stick with it," and I did, and lo and behold, the project changed it all for me.

Bonnie: You have a big dance background. Is that how you started performing in general?

Sarah: Yeah, definitely. I started dancing when I was three, and that led to musical theater as well, which is a combination of it, and performing on stage. My family is so artistic, in that we're either dancers, musicians, actors, painters, or something. Me and my sisters were bound to have that in our systems.

Thomas Doherty

Thomas: When did I know? Yeah, so I grew up in Edinburgh, Scotland. It was a really weird thing. I always wanted to be an actor at the back of my mind. It was always, always there. I watched *Titanic* when I was younger, and I watched Leonardo DiCaprio. He's the most incredible actor, an absolute idol of mine. But I remember watching him when I was seven and thinking, "I could do that." So it was always there, but it wasn't cool.

I feel like nowadays it's quite cool if you want to be an actor or a performer. But back in the day, it wasn't cool, so I was a footballer, or a soccer player. My older brother was a really good soccer player, so we were kind of a soccer family. That was my thing, and I did acting on the side. My mum sent me to these classes.

I left school when I was seventeen. I got all my grades and I thought, I'm either going to waste another year just mucking about at school, or I can do something productive. I was going to audition for acting school, but I didn't think I was mature enough. So I thought, I'll add more strings to my bow. So I'll do musical theater. I did dancing, singing, and acting. All throughout the training, I always knew that I wanted to do acting, so it was kind of redundant that I was doing it, but I still did it.

Bonnie: But you trained, and you're now a true triple threat.

Thomas: Yeah, I suppose you could say that. I guess I can sing and dance and act, hopefully. It's been amazing because my first job I ever got was singing and dancing and acting on *The Lodge*. Then my second job was Harry Hook dancing and rapping. Who knew? The Scottish Eminem. Then *High Strung: Free Dance*, dancing in that. Every job I've done has had dancing and singing in it.

Which is amazing, which is crazy. I'm so grateful. I went to the MGA Academy of Performing Arts in Edinburgh. I'm so grateful for their training and their patience. I think they knew that I wanted to be an actor in ballet class.

Victoria Moroles

Victoria: It's so funny because I have a really hard time thinking about that exact moment when I knew, "I want to be an actor." I feel like I've been performing ever since I was younger, because I've been a dancer since I was three, and we did recitals, a couple recitals every year, so always on that stage.

I dabbled a little bit in musical theater when I was in middle school. I feel like the performing bug has always been in me, but as far as acting goes, I think that it was a period of time where I really found out that I was passionate for it, instead of that one moment of "I have to do this." It was prolonged for sure.

Bonnie: I love that you say that, because there's a lot of confusion around that distinction. There are lots of parents who see their passionate, joyful kids who clearly enjoy performing. And they're normal kids who aren't necessarily meant to be actors for their life's work, but they love performing. And then there is sometimes a total aha moment for some people where they see a certain performance or a certain movie or an actor, and they're like, "Oh my God. That's what I need to do." But then for a lot of actors, it's just sort of that dawning clarity.

Victoria: Exactly. I tried to search for that moment, like, "When was that moment?" I think it's amazing when I hear from friends, "Well, you know, there was this one day," and I think that's so cool that they can remember that. I think that it was just a period of time for me, where I just grew, and grew, and grew every day. I found out that hey, yes, I love performing, but I'm really passionate about acting specifically, and that was probably when I came out here because you don't really know really what it's like until you get out here. I feel like the idea of it is a little bit different than the reality of it.

2

How Did You Get Started?

THERE ARE AS many ways to start an acting career as there are actors, but the stories on the next pages make it clear that the path is rarely straight.

Victoria Moroles signed with an agent at a talent convention and went back and forth to Los Angeles from her native Texas before moving out with her family when she was twelve. It was then several more years before she landed her first role. Luke Benward was cast in his first film at age five, playing Mel Gibson's son in a film that was shooting near his hometown of Nashville, Tennessee.

Sarah Jeffery landed her agent in Vancouver, Canada, when she was young and credits her parents as well as that connection with getting her off to a successful start. Cameron Boyce discovered modeling and commercials through dance class, which then led him to auditioning and acting in films.

Booboo Stewart went with his sister to a singing and dance audition when he was twelve and booked a gig with a Disney group, opening for the Jonas Brothers, Miley Cyrus, and the Cheetah Girls. Dove Cameron got her start acting in community theater when she was eight, but her first TV credit wasn't until she was fifteen.

Thomas Doherty fell in love with acting, dancing, and singing at the age of four, and trained for years in secret to avoid the pain of going against other people's expectations for him. He finally decided to choose what gave him joy, and train openly for it. His first professional TV role, booked at age twenty-one, used all three of those skills, and most of his roles since have too.

Only a couple of these young artists started life in Los Angeles. The rest started in places very far from Hollywood...from the small towns of Rockport, Texas, and Bainbridge Island, Washington, to the cities of Chicago, Detroit, Nashville, Orlando, Union City, Vancouver, and Edinburgh.

Victoria Moroles

Victoria: It's really a long story, but I try to shorten it as much as I can. I feel like my journey kind of started when was about eleven. We actually went to a convention in Dallas.

Bonnie: One of those commercial showcase/ talent convention things?

Victoria: Yeah. I look back and think, "Wow." It was actually more for print and modeling, that specific one, but then they had me do a monologue and the agents were there, and all the jazz and craziness. I found an agent, and I started coming out here, for a couple weeks at a time, and we were just trying to get our feet wet and kind of see what this was about and how I could possibly do it. Then, eventually, we came to the understanding that if I want to do it full time, then I'm going to have to really move out here and be here.

             There are tons of people who come out for seasons, and I did do that, but then you just kind of...I do know people who do tapes and stuff like that and then they still live at home because they want their life at home, and that's completely understandable, but I just felt like I wanted to do it. My grandpa always said, "If you are going to do it, do it one hundred and fifty percent." So we just did it. We moved out here when I was about twelve.

Luke Benward

Luke: My start was a little different than what typically happens. Started acting when I was five, and it kind of fell into place from there. My mom is an acting coach, as you know. It was her agent that called me on my first audition when I was five, living in Nashville, Tennessee. Basically, I booked it that day, and I played Mel Gibson's youngest son in a movie called *We Were Soldiers*.

Bonnie: That's a pretty amazing way to start!

Luke: I didn't see the movie until way after I had grown up and it became age appropriate. It's a rated R film, and a really cool movie, and I didn't even realize it until after. That's where I met my agent who was representing Taylor Momsen at the time—this was right after she was Cindy Lou Who in *The Grinch*.

And then I just continued auditioning and living in Tennessee, going to public school.

Bonnie: Do you remember anything about being five and shooting that movie?

Luke: There are very few things I remember. Because it was shot at Fort Benning in Georgia, they took us to see all the rangers in training, parachuting out of the planes and helicopters. As a kid it was really cool. They took us to boot camp and showed us all the exercises and obstacle courses, so that was really cool too.

I remember Mel Gibson. I remember Mel being really amazing to me as a little five-year-old. I didn't know who he was. I mean I knew who he was, but it didn't matter to me.

I actually remember him doing magic tricks—the illusion where he bent a spoon in front of us. I remember always being on his shoulders. Those are, honestly, most of the memories I have...the young kids in the family wrestling around and being goofy with him.

Bonnie: I love that, because I think it speaks so much to the fact that if you're a five-year-old child actor, you're also five-year-old child. Your experience is going to be the experience of a five-year-old kid like, "Oh, I remember being on his shoulders, I remember seeing the paratroopers." The stuff that would be cool and interesting to a five-year-old is what's interesting to a five-year-old actor.

Luke: Yeah. I really don't think I even realized what I was doing at first. Until I realized that it was a movie and I went and saw a movie, you know what I mean, just because as a kid, you're learning new things all the time.

You're always put in new situations, and you adapt to those situations just because you're learning, and that's just naturally what you do as a child. I think that starting to work so young started that adaptation to the adult world at an earlier part in my life than normal.

Sarah Jeffery

Sarah: It was definitely helpful to have my dad, who's an actor and already had a history in it and knew where to go for it and where not to go. My mom was also extremely helpful. She's a stay-at-home mom, so she had lots of time to help, even though, with that said, it's not easy work.

Bonnie: No, it's a lot of driving to auditions all over town and sitting around forever.

Sarah: Yeah, exactly. It's not easy. I'm extremely grateful that my mom helped me with that. It's headshots; it can be classes; it's auditions, in the morning, at nighttime, sometimes two a day, sometimes none for weeks. Getting started can be a little scary, because you might not be entirely sure, but in my case I found my agent quite young, and she's been with me pretty much from the start, and she's a perfect fit.

Bonnie: Your odds of finding the right connection with an agent the first time out are not super high.

Sarah: I know. I'm so lucky...I have two managers now, one here in LA, one back home, but my one back home in Vancouver has been with me pretty much from the start, and she's been amazing.

Bonnie: That's so huge. That's as important as supportive parents sometimes, for a career.

Sarah: Yeah. You're putting your career into their hands, to a certain degree. It's a collaboration, for sure.

Cameron Boyce

Cameron: I think for me there was a bit of a natural progression. I started as a dancer, and a lot of dancers, because they are performing in a very unique way, and they're entertainers, they get up on stage, and they have to be very vulnerable just like an actor would. Dancers naturally are usually pretty decent actors as well, even at a very raw stage in their acting career. You see a lot of dancers jump to acting, and there are a lot of triple threats, especially on Disney, right? I don't know, it's in our blood a little bit.

A lot of my friends who I danced with from a really young age, they made that jump with me too. I was a dancer, and then I did modeling when I was probably six or seven years old. I did a lot of Disney catalog stuff. I was just jumping around, and smiling, and doing a lot of print. Then that led to commercials. I did about twenty commercials when I was a kid, like sixth grade and fifth grade. There was a point where I would go in, and I would say I probably booked 25 percent of the commercials that I auditioned for.

Bonnie: That's unheard of.

Cameron: For a couple months there, I just booked, and booked, and booked, which is crazy for a seven-year-old kid. I'm like, "I'm on TV a lot. That's crazy."

Bonnie: It's college funds, though.

Cameron: Seriously. My parents were like, "Wow, you're doing good. Nice job." I forget which came first, but I think *Mirrors* was really the first time that I actually acted. Even then I didn't really know what I was doing. I didn't know why I was there. There's no real way to know the gravity of the situation.

I also feel like that's really helped me, because I was so young, and because I didn't really understand the weight of the industry, I just breezed through that part, and I became acclimated in a way that most people don't. A lot of people get thrown into the fire, because they are aware of everything that's going on. For me, I was just like, "Yeah, where do you want me to stand? I'll say this line, and then I'm done? Cool. Free food? Awesome."

That was my experience when I was a kid. And then after a while, I'd done a bunch of movies and stuff, but I think when I realized I wanted to actually be an actor was probably on *Grown Ups*. When I was working with legends at ten years old, and I'm on the set, and Adam Sandler and Kevin James and Chris Rock and David Spade, Rob Schneider, and Maya Rudolph are all on the set with me.

First of all, I didn't know who most of them were, and it was probably better for me to not know that these people are incredible.

Bonnie: Legends.

Cameron: Right. I thought, "Yeah, this is fun," but when I realized that this was something that you had to work at and something that you had to be really conscious at all times about everything that's going on, is when I would do a scene with Sandler and whoever, and because they're these committed geniuses, they would just go off book and not do anything in the script half the time. A ten-year-old kid is waiting for a cue line. I'm waiting for the line before my line, to say my line.

Bonnie: Which never shows up.

Cameron: Right, exactly. Sometimes, they would go off on five-minute tangents in these scenes, and I'm just sitting there, desperately trying not to laugh. I'm watching these ping-pong matches just back and forth, and back and forth with all these jokes, and you have to stay in character. If you don't stay in character, Dennis Dugan, the director comes up and says, "Hey, can you guys stay in character?" That was when I realized that it was going to be something that I couldn't just show up and do.

Bonnie: Yeah, like a print ad.

Cameron: Right, exactly, where you just show up and smile and you're done. For those four months, I'm living in Boston, Massachusetts, at ten years old with my dad, and without my mom and my sister. I'm separated from my life. I'm separated from my friends and school. I'm doing school in trailers. I've started to look around and say, "Wow, this is something that involves a lot." I didn't realize that it was this serious. I didn't realize that it was going to take me completely out of my element, but it did. I really understood, "Wow, this is something that takes a lot more than the average moviegoer thinks."

Bonnie: And you decided you wanted to do it?

Cameron: Yeah. It was easy from there. Even at ten years old, you understand how special it is to really be on a set. When I think back on my time on *Grown Ups* and all these other projects, *Descendants* and *Descendants 2* specifically... they are the spaces that just breathe creative life and everything just circulates in it. It's really a very special place to be, and going from that back to public school was the rudest awakening. I would go back and then feel like, "Wow, I don't want to be here. I want to be back on set." That's where I really realized that this is a special thing that I get to do that not everyone gets to do. I just ran with it from there.

Honestly, I'm all of the stereotypes. I'm everything. I'm a Disney kid, I'm a child actor, I'm all these things. I think there are really two differences. The first one is the kid has to want to be there. My parents were really skeptical about it. It's one of those things where you think, "Oh, child actors become terrible people and that's just how it goes."

But there are so many child actors who we don't talk about, because they didn't end up crazy, and because they're not in the tabloids, we say, "Where are they?" It's like, "They're working in a cubicle." They are regular people.

Bonnie: They're having a life.

Cameron: Yeah, exactly. So the first thing is that for me, I grew up, and I still wanted to do it. In fact, a lot of kids grow up and realize, "Wow, I didn't have a choice before, because

I was so young, and now that I see the industry for what it really is, I don't really like it." That's totally natural and normal, and that happens so often.

I think what helps kids like me who actually do want to do it, and what turns kids off to the industry most of the time, and there's a very thin line, is the parents. The parents really are everything. As a kid, all you want to do, it doesn't matter what you're doing as a kid, if that is going to make your parents happy, you want to do well.

If a parent goes to a kid and says, "Okay, I want you to stand on this mark, and you're going to say this line with a lot of energy, and you're going to do it right, and you're going to impress the director, and it's going to be great." All that kid wants to do now is do what you just said and impress not the director, not anybody else who would watch the movie, but just their parent. That's it. That's all it is. For a kid, it's like that in everything. Like a basketball parent says, "Make your free throws and dribble the ball correctly, and don't travel and don't double dribble." That's what the kid wants to do. He just wants to be good at basketball, because that's what the parent is asking of them.

Bonnie: Dance, baseball, you name it.

Cameron: Everything. We talk about "stage parents," but a parent can be overbearing in any scenario that I just mentioned or you just mentioned—baseball and basketball and all the sports and all of the theater and anything. A parent can be overbearing in anything. I think the thing that really messes child actors up is a parent wants a kid to be really good at something, sometimes for different reasons. A parent will want their kid to be really good at baseball, because they want their kid to be a good athlete. Maybe they won't make the MLB, but they want them to be good at it, right?

A lot of times with a child actor and a stage parent, the stage parent's motivation for their child to be an actor is, "Oh, my kid is going to be famous."

They're going to have all the money, and they're going to pay me, and my son's going to buy me a house and a car and all the stuff. That is the completely wrong approach. Every stage parent who has ever put their child into acting for that reason, once the child becomes twelve or thirteen and understands what's going on around them and why their parent wants them to be in it, they're immediately disgusted by it. They're turned off, they don't want to do it anymore, and they quit.

Bonnie: Yes, and it wrecks their relationship, which is a tragedy.

Cameron: Completely. It's the worst of every situation. That's the last thing that you want. When we talk about child actors, for me, I really like to dance. I would always go to dance class, and then all of my friends were doing commercials and doing stuff like that. I went to my parents and said, "What is that? Let's do that. That looks fun," and we did that. Then it just grew from there. My parents were just as skeptical as any other regular parent would be about it. They said, "Listen, if you ever end up hating this, if you ever don't like it, if you ever don't feel like doing it anymore, then we stop." This is what you want, because it's your career, it's your life, it's your childhood. That's what is at stake here. This is all a risk, all of this. It's all up in the air.

They were saying, "Listen, a lot of things come with this life." You know what I mean? I've learned at this point that I'm down a road that I can't turn back on. I can't turn around and go the other way. It doesn't happen.

Even if I stop acting right now, I will get recognized on the street. I will still get attention. I will still have the followers that I do. It's just, I'm already down the road, you know what I mean? They understood that when I was a young kid. They would say to me, "If this is something that you don't want to do, then we're going to stop." They kept me in public school for as long as they could. Once I booked *Jessie*, I couldn't, because you're on set five days a week, but I was a regular kid for the longest.

I think because my parents brought me up that way as opposed to having an ego trip and thinking that they were getting some glory from their kid's projects and stuff, it really benefited me and I've grown out of that with a really good understanding of why things happen the way they do in this industry.

Booboo Stewart

Booboo: It was kind of a fluid transition because I was already dancing. Once we figured out that I wanted to act, my dad just started asking around. Asking if I could do little bit parts here and there. I just started auditioning. It's always an interesting thing, getting started. Friends ask me, "How do I get an agent?" and things. It's such a catch-22. There's no real way.

Bonnie: There's also every way, which is the other way to look at it. Every way and no way.

Booboo: Yeah, it's the weirdest thing, getting started, trying to pinpoint how it happened. I don't know. I just started doing stunts. Working with my dad.

Bonnie: You were also modeling when you were a kid, right?

Booboo: Yeah, I was. That's what I'm saying. I was doing stunts, and then I just started auditioning for commercials. You start auditioning for random photo shoots with Target and stuff like that. I got really lucky with Hot Wheels. I was doing music. I think it was my older sister who had an audition for this Disney group, and I ended up going, and they asked me to audition, so it's one of those things.

I auditioned and got that. Then I started touring with the Disney group. I was twelve.

Bonnie: You were twelve years old, and you were opening for the Jonas Brothers?

Booboo: Jonas Brothers were just becoming famous. I don't know if you remember, it was "Year 3000," that kind of era for the Jonas Brothers. Super early. Then with Miley Cyrus and the Cheetah Girls who were really famous at the time.

Bonnie: You're opening and touring with them?

Booboo: Yeah. We did the Staples Center. It's kind of weird. Getting started, I guess, was just such a natural thing because I was so enveloped inside of the business already.

Bonnie: You were dancing too.

Booboo: I was dancing too. In the Disney group, I danced.

Bonnie: That's amazing. That's so cool. I love it when guys are into dance especially. It's such a classic thing for girls to be interested in dance when they're kids, but there aren't as many guys who really enjoy and appreciate dance.

Booboo: No, and that's the thing too. If you're a young guy and you're listening to this, start dancing because if you want to start working, there aren't a lot of guy dancers. I don't think I'm that good of a dancer, but because I have a different look and because there weren't a lot of guy dancers, and I was just a child, I really worked a lot. I trained really hard too, but you know what I mean. It helps if you go to an open call for dancing for the *Kid's Choice Awards*, being a back-up dancer...if there's two hundred girls, there's like seventy-five guys.

Bonnie: So your odds are so much better.

Booboo: It's so much better. I danced a lot for Brian Friedman, Hi-Hat, some of the top choreographers. Did all the Macy's Passport. I guess the more you do, the more people you meet and the more work you can come by because you know people.

Bonnie: It's really true. Work does beget work, and every time you work with somebody new, if you like each other and it goes well, that tends to open more doors for the future.

Booboo: Yeah. Especially in stunts and dancing and modeling. You go in and you know the photographer, if you're doing a photo shoot. That's helps. You know the clients. If you're dancing, you know the choreographer, which is 50 percent of the battle…it's a weird thing.

Bonnie: Well, it's not too weird though because a lot is at stake on all of these projects, and everybody knows that they need somebody that they can count on. Who's going to actually show up and do the work and be easy and pleasant to work with, you know? Every time you try somebody new, it's a wild card.

That whole, "It's who you know," cliché, well, there's some truth to that, but it's for a good reason.

Booboo: That is very true. If you're not good at your job, or you just don't put in the time or the work, it doesn't matter who you know if they can't trust that you're going to be able to be there then.

Bonnie: Word does get out. It does go both ways. I was talking to Victor Boyce, Cameron's dad, and he said that you and Cameron were in a dance class together at some point.

Booboo: When we were really young. I don't know how old I was. Maybe twelve or something. Oh, maybe younger than that because Cameron was really, really young. Yeah, we were in the same dance company together. A lot of dance classes together. We used to dance at Millennium Dance Center; then our company moved.

Bonnie: I love that. And then to see you guys working together on *Descendants* is so...

Booboo: So random (laughing).

Bonnie: It's beautiful though, right?

Booboo: It's amazing. Yeah. It really is cool to see us now...because at that age, you wouldn't hang out, because of your age differences, so much. Now I love Cameron. He's the man.

Thomas Doherty

Thomas: My best friend, Ronan Burns, we were born a month apart, and we kind of grew up as children together. Went to the same primary schools, which is elementary here?

He was very into theater, musicals. You know, when you're younger, you kind of send your son or daughter to whatever your friend's son or daughter is doing. So I went, not really having any idea what I was doing. I mean you don't really know when you're four what's going on, so I just went. It was in an old church, which is now a mosque. I didn't know what I was doing, I didn't know why I was doing it, I just did it. I also sometimes think that because my brother was the much better soccer player, and the attention was on him for being the soccer player, I was like, "What's my thing? I want my own thing, I want my own niche."

So I gradually did that. All through primary school I did various different kinds of theater schools and stage schools, and little plays and stuff. Then when I got to high school…in Scotland, primary school is from grade one to seven. That's like five years old to twelve.

Then high school is twelve years old to eighteen, and that's it. Then you go to college or university. So you don't have a middle school or anything. I went to high school, and like I said earlier, it wasn't cool to be doing this. So I went to dance class in secret.

It was like a Billy Elliot story. I went to the MGA Academy Theater School twice a week, and I'd go to school, normal school, and be this footballing guy, this cool guy, or rather I thought I was.

Bonnie: Being cool is so important at that age. It's like wearing… Dove and I used to call it "camo." When you're putting on your camouflage clothes, you're trying to look like everybody else so that you can blend in and survive. It's about survival.

Thomas: It is a survival thing. I think it's a Japanese saying…If you're the nail that sticks out, you'll get hammered.

Bonnie: That's what school feels like at a certain age, and it can be terrorizing. So you were hiding; you were being Billy Elliot.

Thomas: I was. So I'd have my schoolbag, and I'd have my book, textbooks, jotters, and things, and I'd have my lunch. At the bottom of my bag, I'd have a leotard, tights, tap shoes, ballet shoes. It was just this big secret, nobody knew. Everybody at MGA, at the theater school, knew that it was a big secret. I did that for four years in secret.

Bonnie: A double life.

Thomas: It was crazy. Even in the house, I wouldn't play musical theater songs, in case my dad or my brother...It
was just ridiculous, because they were the most supportive people. When they came to the shows, they'd
say, "That's amazing, I love that." My dad told me, "I'm
so proud of you. This is amazing. This is incredible. You
can get up on that stage and do it in front of all these
people." I had a lot of friends, like my best friend, and
my girlfriend at the time, their dads were macho; they
were disapproving of it, for boys anyway. I thought my
family would be the same, when they were the complete opposite.

But I kept it quiet for all these years, and then my close
friends at school kind of found out when I was about fifteen, sixteen. But it was only exclusively acting.

Bonnie: They didn't know that you also loved to dance and sing.

Thomas: No, no, no. I played soccer at a club outside of school as
well. On Saturday mornings, at nine o'clock, I'd have singing for an hour, ballet, jazz, acting, each for an hour. So
four hours on a Saturday morning. Run upstairs to the
toilets, get changed out of my leotards, get my football
bag out, get changed into my football kit. Put my shin
guards and my football boots on, run downstairs, get
into the car, my mum would be waiting every Saturday.
Take me to the football game, I'd jump out, and every
week they'd ask, "Why are you late?" And I'd say, "Traffic."
I'd be sweating from the dancing, and I'd just run on the
pitch and play football. No one knew.

Oh my God, it was so stressful. I think I had a heart attack when I was fourteen, when I forgot my bag on the bus and all my dance stuff was in there. I figured it was over— I'd need to move schools, leave the country.

It was the biggest thing, it was such a big thing. Then when I'd finished my exams...and I had a year left of school, everyone kind of found out.

I survived, but when they found out, it was so embarrassing. Then I started going to theater school, having this macho kind of thing, because I was like no, I'm not gay.

Yeah, that's what you get slagged at school. "Oh, you're gay. Gays do that." That was the last year. Then when I was thinking about leaving school, that was also playing in my mind. I thought, "I like doing this. This is fun. Is their opinion really more important than what I want to do, what makes me happy? What's fun to me?" Then I realized it wasn't.

Bonnie: I think if everybody could make that distinction, the world would be a much happier place. Like, wait a minute, what's actually important here? Their opinion of me, or my happiness?

Thomas: I think it's a bit morbid, but when you introduce your mortality, your impending death, which is deemed as such a bad thing...but death is what makes life so precious, without it, it'd be kind of nothing. When you think about that, you realize, do I want to live my life for other people, like they're doing? Or do I want to do what makes me happy? When you kind of weigh it up, it's a no-brainer.

Bonnie: It is a no-brainer, and I'm so happy that you were able to come to that wise conclusion at the age of sixteen or seventeen.

Thomas: It's a gradual process as well; it's not like, "That's it." It's always a gradual process, and it evolves and it changes, and it becomes different things. Once you're comfortable with this, you'll then become comfortable with one thing, but then...it's an ever-going kind of process, I guess.

            But I do genuinely believe that there is a point in which the process finishes. Where you become disassociated with your accumulated mind, your ego, then it doesn't become an issue. I do think there is a point, and I'm definitely not there yet.

            That is honestly a goal in my life, to achieve that. If I can act along the way, that sounds good.

Bonnie: It's a good goal. I was talking with a choreographer, Paul Becker, and he said basically if you're a guy who can dance, your odds of success are just so huge, because there are so few guys who can dance because of this silly stigma. They just don't let themselves even try it.

Thomas: It's mad.

Bonnie: If you're a good dancer, your odds of getting work are really pretty decent, if you're a guy. Whereas, there's a zillion girls who love to dance, and the competition's a lot thicker there.

Thomas: Yeah, even if you didn't want to dance, just getting into your body, and being able to understand the way your body moves, and being able to manipulate the way your body moves, that's also a fantastic thing. So you might explicitly want to be an actor, but I'd strongly, strongly recommend dancing in any capacity. Or yoga, or just something to get into your body.

Bonnie: You took singing lessons too, right?

Thomas: Yeah, I did. I mean I'm not the best singer in the world, but I did do them.

It makes such a difference. You start to understand your breathing a bit more, and you'll be surprised the amount of auditions you'll go to and they'll be like, "Can you sing?" You need to be able to say yeah. Now it's not even triple threats, it's quadruple threats. People ask, "Can you play an instrument? Can you play two instruments?" So yeah, the more strings to your bow you have, the more likelihood you have of booking.

Bonnie: It's really true. I tell young actors that all the time, and if you can be genuinely decent, maybe even really good at some other stuff, you could get cast.

That's how Dylan Playfair got his start, playing hockey players. He was already a really good hockey player, of course. You can't start from scratch.

Thomas: No way, you've got to build from something. So the more exposure, the more experience you have is good.

Bonnie: Plus it makes for a richer life. It's not just all about utility. That's a terrible way to live your life. It's cynical.

Thomas: It's doing something for something else, as opposed to just doing it.

Bonnie: Yes, for the joy, for the richness.

Thomas: For the joy. That happened to me, and I realized I'm going to get to seventy, and I'll have just been living my life two steps ahead, forever living for the two steps ahead. It's a long life as well. I mean, you are going to die, but it's also a long life. You need to enjoy it.

Dove Cameron

Dove: Typically when children ask me, "When did you start acting?" I will say theater because that's usually what they have access to, and that's true. I want them to take theater seriously in terms of a training ground. It is honestly just much easier to get into community theater than it is to get into, sort of, the Hollywood circles. Simply because there are just more community theaters than there is a Hollywood.

Bonnie: There's a community theater in almost every community, whereas you basically have to come to Los Angeles to have access to Hollywood.

Dove: Right, and so if kids ask, "Hey, how did you get your start?" I want to give them a piece of advice that they can put into action, because obviously they're asking me for a reason. If I say I started in community theater, which is true, it can sometimes inspire them to enroll in community theater, and I've gotten a lot of kids telling me that. They say, "I started in community theater because of you, and I'm hoping to become an actor like you."

If an industry professional asks, "When did you start?" I'm probably going to say my first TV credit.

Bonnie: Which was not until you were fifteen.

Dove: Right, and so it depends on who's asking, and both are real answers.

What was it like for these young actors to land in Hollywood? Who inspires them? How do they stay focused on their dreams when the going gets tough? What would they do if they weren't actors?

Go to https://bonniejwallace.com/bonus-chapters/ to download these *free bonus chapters* that weren't included in the final manuscript due to length issues.

3

Finding an Agent or Manager

SIGNING WITH AN agent or manager is one of the biggest milestones for an actor's career. While it's true that you can get work as an actor without an agent or manager, auditions for desirable roles in LA or New York can only be accessed through an agent, and just getting the attention of a decent talent agent is a triumph.

There are three basic ways to sign with an agent or manager:

1. Headshot and Résumé Method

    This method basically consists of sending in your headshot and résumé with a cover letter and hoping the agent or manager will call you in for a meeting. This can work in smaller markets but rarely works in the bigger ones. Better talent agents and managers in the major markets generally only meet with potential clients through referrals and rarely look at unsolicited requests for meetings.

2. Referrals

    Referrals from a trusted source in the industry (another agent, manager, director, producer, acting coach, etc.) can result in a meeting. This only works if the person making the referral can genuinely speak for the talent and readiness of the actor as well as has the respect and trust of the agent or manager they are making the referral to. That's a lot of stars to align, but it can happen.

3. Showcases

    Showcases where an actor can perform for agents and managers who are looking for new talent constitute the most common way that actors get reps, and there are many different kinds of showcases. Some cost many thousands of dollars, provide thin training, and don't typically lead to great results, as most of the performers just aren't ready to work professionally. Others are presented by respected acting schools or university programs, and can cost several hundred dollars, or years of tuition, but because the actors actually have some solid training, they tend to be more successful.

    These young actors found their agents through all three of these methods. It's good to remember that just because you get a meeting with an agent or a manager, it doesn't mean that you will sign with them. They may think you aren't ready yet. Or they may think you are amazing, but they already have too many actors in your "type."

    Even if you sign with an agent or manager, your journey is just beginning. But signing with one marks the beginning of the next phase of your journey...

Dove Cameron

Dove: I remember that my mom did a lot of work. I remember I got headshots first, and we sent them in to a couple—I think we only sent them in to three agencies? I've had the same agent since I moved here when I was fourteen. I haven't had to find a new one because Pam Fisher is so incredible, and I'm still with Abrams Youth Theatrical—yay, baby face! I haven't had to find a new one, and I really don't want to. If I didn't ever have to leave my agent, I would be very happy.

I do know that just sending your picture in with your résumé will pretty much guarantee it gets put in the trash can. Again, I'm speaking very candidly, and I'm sorry if it's coming off as harsh. I don't mean it to. I just want to be as helpful as possible, and I do believe the truth is helpful.

If you send in your photo with a résumé, too many come in per day, per week, per month, and they just throw them away. Any big agent would tell you the same, because they don't have the time or the manpower to look into everybody, to call everybody in. That would just be taking endless meetings, and then their client list that they already have wouldn't get any attention.

Finding a good agent is definitely difficult. You start out with someone who will kind of take anyone, because those are the ones who will take your call, because if you don't have any references or connections or any previous work, the only people who will take you are the people who are starting at the bottom. That's not a comment on your talent or your looks or anything. Jessica Lange had no work on her résumé when she first started, so I don't mean that in a personal way. I just mean that you have to start somewhere. You've got to start at the bottom and then work your way up through agencies, I've heard, by proving yourself and kicking booty on your auditions and booking stuff and all that.

It definitely does help to have connections. It sounds really shady when I say that, but otherwise an agent won't know...if you have somebody who can call in and vouch for your talent, an agent would take that much more seriously. It's sad, but it's definitely true. I don't remember what we did.

Bonnie: That's about what happened. We were getting nowhere with the whole sending in the headshot thing. It had been months. I was starting to really worry, and I called the one industry contact we had who was someone who had directed you and coached you.

Dove: In community theater, by the way.

Bonnie: That's right, and she had been one of your mentors that said I should take you seriously as a talent and come to LA.

Dove: Shout out to you, Dinah Manoff! You are the MVP, Dinah Manoff.

Bonnie: She really is. I called her and said, "I don't know what to do. We are getting nowhere. I think I might have made a mistake by coming down here without an agent." She asked who we were looking at, and I gave her the three names, which was, of course, crazy and ambitious already. She knew one. She made a phone call. Then we got a phone call, and you had a meeting scheduled with Pamela Fisher within fifteen minutes. It was incredible.

Dove: So it's really hard to get a good agent, you guys. It's really hard. It's like finding a good, straight boyfriend. It's like finding a good man. I feel like I'm in *Steel Magnolias*.

Bonnie: But it's a relationship.

Dove: It is, but then also you have the meeting. Then you have to razzle-dazzle. I remember I went all over town to find the right shoes to meet my potential agent. I got all dressed up and then had to get that monologue all memorized. I actually do remember that. I remember that meeting very vividly. Oh gosh, I was terrified. I was so nervous. I think I was beet red. I was just blushing so hard, and I was so scared. Because we had waited for months.

It's like an audition. Once you get the meeting, there's no dancing around, and it's not like "You're fine. They'll love you no matter what." You've got to really fight for it because they've got a long client list, and one thing that a lot of people won't tell you about Hollywood—it's sad, but it's true—if you have a similar face to somebody that they already have on their roster, even if you're the most talented kid or person in the world, they might not take you just based on that.

Because so many breakdowns these days are "calling for a five-foot-three; long, black hair; big eyes" or "calling for a six-foot-seven blonde, tan," so many are based on physical attributes. You can be an Oscar-worthy performer, and some agencies just might not take you because they already have someone who's your type. It can be very hard. There's kind of no getting around that. You've just got to keep going to different agencies until you find a place that you fit.

Bonnie: Yes, and then as you said, maybe make your way up over time.

Dove: Exactly. This is kind of terrifying, but if you treat every single experience like a test, I used to tell myself that—which is a little scary for a fourteen-year-old to be like "everything is a test"—but I would. I would imagine that every single room that I walked into was like taking a test. Like taking a math test or something. I would try to ace every single one. I would try to do every single thing right because it's bettering your chances. It's like putting more tickets into the jar...you know, when people are drawing tickets, if you put in eight, you're more likely to get one pulled than if you put in one. You just do as much as you can, as best as you can, for as long as you can, and you'll succeed.

Garrett Clayton

Garrett: When I came out here, I met with the manager after I emailed him about four times...In the last one, I said, "If you don't want to meet, that's fine, but I'm very serious about what I'm doing, and I'm going to find someone else to represent me if you won't. So if I don't hear back from this email, I'm going to move forward without you."

Bonnie: Wow!

Garrett: Then I got a big, "Ha, ha, ha, ha," back, and he said, "Are you free Wednesday?" I went, and I met with all the managers there. Again, feeling very *42nd Street*, where you show up and it's this big building and the name is across the top and you're in Beverly Hills and you go to the top floor and you see the view and this giant, beautiful conference room that's all glass-window walls.

He asked, "What is your goal? What's your plan?" I said, "Well, I want to be an actor." He goes, "What kind of an actor do you want to be? Who do you want to be? What you need to do is you need a six-month plan, a year plan, a five-, and a ten-year plan. Who do you want to be in ten years? What do you want to accomplish in five years? What's the point when you know you're midway to where you need to get?"

Bonnie: Right. How do you know you're on track?

Garrett: So, I said, "I don't know." I just barely turned nineteen, and I don't even...I'm three thousand miles away from home, and I don't know...The last place I lived was my parents' house.

So, he says, "Well, to start, within the first six months, you need a job, a car, somewhere to live, which you've already done, and acting classes. So once you have steady acting classes and you have some way to get to them, to do the things you need to do, and some way to supplement your income so you can stay, then come talk to me."

So I found a job the first day, because I told myself I wasn't allowed to go home until I found a job.

Bonnie: Wow. What kind of job? Can I ask?

Garrett: I was a waiter at a twenty-four-hour restaurant for two years. I started waiting at IHOP when I was fifteen, sixteen. I got the signed letter from my parents and the school saying that I could.

Bonnie: So, you were experienced. That's an important thing. I mean, in LA especially, you don't just walk in and say, "I'd like to..."

Garrett: People want you to come in with some waiting experience. If you can say, "I know how to wait on tables," they'll say, "Okay. Yeah. All right. Well, that's what we need."

Bonnie: For people who are thinking about coming to LA, maybe after high school or whatever, and maybe paying the rent through being a waiter or something, get some experience before you leave home.

Garrett: Oh, completely. That'll help...When I got my job in LA, it was after me getting very frustrated, and I walked into this twenty-four-hour coffee shop restaurant, and I said, "Do you need any more people to work here, because I need a job, and I don't have time to mess around. I just need to know if you are hiring or not. I don't want to fill out another application if you're not hiring."

She says, "Okay. Well, I think the owner's going to like you. Yeah. Hold on. Just wait an hour. Can you wait an hour?" I was like, "Yeah. I don't have anything else to do."

So I found a job the first day. I got a car in a week, and then I got acting classes the second week, and then a month later, I found myself an agent.

Bonnie: Wow! So now, how did you find the agent? You had the manager, kind of.

Garrett: It was through a vocal coach that was at my program who, when he was in school, he knew this guy who's an agent out here now. The play I'm doing now is through a coach, I'd done his workshops, and I've known the director for years, and they just needed a guy that was my age and type.

A lot of things in this town, it's just cultivating good relationships. If you work really hard and you're really dedicated, I think people don't forget that.

Cameron Boyce

Cameron: I was six or seven, I guess. My friends were doing it, and they had agents, I'm sure. I just let my parents handle it, but what they would tell you is they just went online probably and researched good kid's agencies. We found an agent. I guess we contacted them somehow. I ended up doing an interview with them. They just wanted to see me in person and know what I was like and see if I had personality and things like that. Again, I was a kid. I don't really remember what I did to impress them, but I was just being myself. I think a lot of kids are really shy when they're around people they don't know, but you can tell when a kid would be a good actor, because they just don't care. They just continue to be themselves, and they'll talk to whoever, and they're super outgoing. I guess I was that kid.

They signed me, and things took off from there. Everybody has a different experience. I know people who love a certain agent, and I'll talk to somebody else who hates the same person and loves a certain manager and somebody else who hates the same person. That confused me for so long. It's like, "Okay, how could they be great and terrible at the same time?" I don't get it. I think the most important thing, and the thing that we were really lucky to find with Osbrink, which was my first agency, was for whatever reason they really cared about me.

Sometimes, agencies take on people that they don't really have the time for or they're not really super passionate about. They just took them on for whatever reason. That's when you get the stories like, "Oh, they do nothing. They do absolutely nothing." Then you talk to somebody else, and they say, "I've had five auditions this week. They're doing great."

Bonnie: Yes, and it's the same agent.

Cameron: It's the same agent. The most important thing is finding somebody who is passionate about you. I was able to find that with Osbrink. I had a manager back when I was nine years old, who did nothing. I booked something that she had no part in; there was nothing that she did to help. She said, "Wait, where's my ten percent?" And we said, "You're still working for us?" We didn't even remember. That stuff happens. Now, I have a better understanding of it, and I've switched agents pretty recently. Again, the most important thing for me is somebody who cares about me and also really understands what I want and where I'm coming from.

Because when I was seven, I had no vision of where I wanted my career to go. Now, I have a very good idea. When I explain that and somebody can say, "Oh, and this also...what about that?" and I can say, "Yeah, that's exactly what I want. That's exactly what I hadn't thought of, but you just thought of it, and I'm so down for it." That's when you feel a connection, and you end up signing. Then they take it from there. I still don't have a manager. I am with an agency. I have a publicist, but I get auditions from my agent. I'm sure eventually I'll probably have a manager. Just do what's best for you.

Whatever feels right, whichever person feels the most passionate who means business and will get you what you need—that's the person that you go with. But I've always gone with my gut. That's so important. Just go with what you feel. Everybody says, "Oh, this person's bad" or "Oh, this person's good." You've got to block out that noise and just say, "Hey, this is the person I'm gravitating toward, so that's who I'm running with."

Bonnie: You've got to go with your gut, because in my experience, every time I've gone against my gut instincts, I have regretted it without exception.

Cameron: Yeah, same here. I've felt weird or awkward or bad about certain things, but somebody would tell me, "No, this is good for you." Then I'd do it. Then I'd look back and think, "No, that's not good for me. I didn't want to do that. It didn't feel right," so you've got to go with your gut really. That's the most important thing.

Bonnie: It's really hard to go wrong if you're doing it...and super easy to go wrong if you don't.

Cameron: And even if it was the wrong decision, you still don't regret it, because you've felt a certain way about it. You

should always go with your gut. That's the most important thing.

Thomas Doherty

Thomas: At the MGA school they do a showcase every year. That's
            down in London, and they can invite people over. It's a
            fantastic opportunity for agents to suss you out a little
            bit, see your look, see what your abilities are. So it's a
            good thing. Then you'll go on for more meetings and
            stuff. But you might get two minutes of singing, five min-
            utes of dancing, maybe a two-minute scene. So it's not
            a lot, it's only a taster. So fear not, if you're not going to
            one of these institutions, because it doesn't really mat-
            ter. It's really six of one and half a dozen of the other. But
            if you don't go to one of these schools, my advice would
            be to suss out agents, send some emails to agents ask-
            ing, saying that you want representation.

            Don't go for the big guns at first, if you've had no expe-
            rience. If you want a booking (theatrical) agent, I would
            strongly recommend that you make a show reel. There
            are classes all the time for show reels. Even YouTube.
            You can get a little flavor for how to make a show reel or
            what show reels look like. You know, you'd say, "I don't
            have anything. I've never been in anything to put in my
            show reel." But you can get some monologues from films
            that you really like or some monologues that are in your
            range of castability and you sit down and you just do a
            self-tape. You do a couple of self-tapes; don't make it
            too long, because they'll get bored. Yeah, you just film
            yourself. Make sure it's a clear backdrop. I'm sure they all
            know the shebang about how to make a self-tape.

Film from the chest up. Good lighting and good audio. Clear background, and you can just make your own little show reel. You can do as many takes as you want, and fire your headshots out as well. Someone will see your look and see some potential. That's all it takes, just for someone to see you. Then you never know, but until that happens, which it will happen, just keep pushing, keep trying, and keep working on yourself. Both in the industry, and in reality, normal life. Keep doing that, keep learning, and keep growing.

Jessica Marie Garcia

Jessica: I was lucky. I got my agent through that horrible manager. And when I left her, I thought my agent would leave me, but we just got another manager who was better. Not much better but legally better. She was technically better. She wasn't doing anything illegal, but then what I then fell into was being the best...I'm sorry to be this blunt but to be the best actor in a group of child actors.

I was still older. I'm someone who's older who plays younger. As far as training went, I was so far past them and she would have me do showcase after showcase and the people I was meeting would say, "I don't understand why you're here." That turned into feeling I'm just throwing my money away because I'm not going out on auditions. I'm just having a bunch of people tell me I'm good, and that does nothing for me.

Then when I left her, she told me, "Oh, I just didn't think you were serious about this." I said, "How could you possibly think that?" I'm training and training and training, getting ready for the day that I'm auditioning for something, but I'm not getting those auditions. Then luckily I had a friend who I lived with who had been with that horrible manager. She worked as a commercial agent, and she got me a meeting with Pam Fisher. Meeting Pam Fisher completely changed my life. It's all who you know, and it's all being in that right room, at the right time.

Bonnie: You were ready too.

Jessica: I was ready.

Bonnie: That's the thing. There are a lot of ways to hold that whole "It's who you know" thing, and a lot of people are really bitter about that because they feel like if you don't know anybody, you're shut out.

Jessica: If you use that as an excuse, then you're not writing your own content, and you're not getting out there because you will meet them if you do that. That's just a lazy person's way of being upset about something like that because you have to be in the right rooms. I got myself in the right rooms. You know what I mean?

Bonnie: You got yourself there. Then when you got in that room, you were ready, and that's the second piece of that.

It may sometimes be who you know, but that won't take you anywhere if you don't have what it takes to go somewhere with that. You did at that point and then some. That's exciting. Then, of course, now you've got Pam Fisher.

Jessica: I know. God bless. I had no idea what an agent was supposed to do or how it was supposed to be in this business. I learned so much of the business through her because she educated me. She wasn't just blindly submitting me. She got to know who I was and what I wanted and where I wanted my career to go, then told me, "This is how you get there." You need an agent who works for you. You can have a great agent.

I've had friends who are great actors who have had agents who scream at them and yell at them and are not available. I wouldn't want an agent who is that way, but some people do. Some people just want to know where they have to go and don't want to get to know them, but I love the fact that I can call my manager or agent and just say, "You know what, I had a really bad audition. I just need to talk about it." They'll sit there with me and talk to me about it. I need that. Some people don't. You have to find somebody who works for you.

Bonnie: I think back to your previous point about being far and away the best of the talent that your previous agent had. That's not a good thing. It's not a good thing to be the top client, the most successful talent of your agent or manager.

If you're at the top, you probably want to be somewhere else.

And if you're at the bottom, you probably aren't getting the attention you need. You want to find an agent or a manager where there's a fit that makes sense, where who you are makes sense with the other people that they're representing and that they're sending out.

Jessica: Or they at least care about you enough to really pitch you. I have friends who had great agents but, again, like you said, they were low on the totem pole, so the agents didn't know how to pitch them. That's horrible. It's like, "Oh, you could have gotten me this audition. Did you pitch me?"

"How would you pitch me? Tell me how would you pitch me?" If they don't know how to do that, then they probably don't believe in you, and you need someone who believes in you."

Victoria Moroles

Victoria: I was just trying to think of how many agents I've had. That's really sad.

Bonnie: Here is the thing that's great about that, that I want people to notice: there is a lot of drama and stress around just getting in front of an agent ever, to even have the possibility of having them want to sign with you. Then even when you do, there is typically a time when it's time to change and get somebody else because you've maybe grown out of them or they are not what you hoped they would be or whatever. There is every reason. Then there is a whole other stress that goes on that's like, "I'll never get another agent again," and it feels so personal. It's like breaking up with a boyfriend, right?

Victoria: Yes. I know that feeling to the teeth. I'm with CESD now, and I came out here when I was twelve. I had that agent, and then I switched around maybe, I think about three times with agents, different agents. I've had a couple of different managers. I've been with CESD for about five years. I've been with them for a good amount of time. I love CESD. I love all of my agents. You find somebody who believes in you and you believe in them; it goes both ways.

That's the thing that I feel like a lot of people get caught up in and are so nervous about. You are both finding each other. They want you, and you want them. Yes, of course, you are joining their agency, and you kind of have a little bit more of the pressure. But not really because once you get to the point where I'm at, if I'm not having auditions, it's fifty-fifty, it really is.

And I think it's like this preconceived notion of, you are going into a big agency, and you should be really nervous. If you realize that they are there for you as much as you are there for them, it makes you feel a little bit better. I'm actually out of a manager right now.

It's my first time being in between managers. I thought I always needed to have an agent and a manager. If something is not working out for you, why continue that? I have a hard time making big decisions like that. And now I just have my agency. It's okay. If somebody comes along that you feel like you connect with, by all means, but don't feel like you need to have both of those all the time. I definitely think you need to have one of them.

Bonnie: You do need an agent in California and New York because managers aren't allowed by law to get actors work. They aren't licensed and bonded like agents are. There is that little thing.

The other thing is where you are personally in your career right now is not where you were a few years ago. You've got a lot more credits under your belt. The kind of manager that you'll be able to attract now is not the kind of manager you could have found a couple years ago.

Victoria: I also can have a hard time with how closely you work with managers. Yes, it is business, but if they don't understand you, it's really hard, because they deal with all of the things that the agents don't hear about and the calls… I'm running late, and I need to schedule this and that, and the personal issues. If they don't like connecting with you on that level, at least for me, it's hard. Other people, they can kind of keep it business, but I need somebody who I can just be straight up with.

Bonnie: I think it's a very personal relationship. Ideally.

Victoria: Exactly. Ideally, that is really what you want.

Dylan Playfair

Dylan: I think a lot of actors forget that when you do get an agent, they work for you. That's a weird position to get your head around because leading up to that, you're thinking, "God, if I could just get an agent…" You're coming in asking them to support you, to take a risk.

Bonnie: The power is on their side.

Dylan: They have all the power, but then once that happens, you've got to go in your head and say, "Now it's a team. Now we're working together." They're on your payroll in a sense. They take a percentage of what you make, and they want you to work, and you want to work.

To answer your question, the first agent and still the same agent I have is Carrie Wheeler. I signed with her through Jared Kesso, who was the hockey player I met playing B league after getting on the set as a PA through Silvan Harper. It was really just asking people questions and saying, "I don't know how to get started, but I want to get started. Can you help me out?" When I found out that he was another actor, I said the same thing. It wasn't right away that he offered that up. He watched me take classes for months before he said, "You know what? Call this girl. She'll help you."

He'd done the same thing. He had come out from back east, and he was a hockey player, and he got into acting, and...people want to help. I think people are inherently good, and I think people, when they see someone who is passionate about something they are passionate about, they really want to help you out. I think film is cool in that sense. I think a lot of people think you're on the outside of something, but it's shocking to see how helpful people really want to be. It makes them feel good to know they've given back and helped someone up the ladder. That for me was Jared Kesso.

Bonnie: I agree completely. That's been our experience as well. It's not what people think it's like. This seems to be the experience for a lot of people.

Dylan: I think people get a misconception that it's mean and hard and cold and you only get respect once you're massive. It's really not that way. People love what they do, and I think they recognize they're lucky to do it, and they want to share that feeling with other people. It's a really rewarding thing to know that your words or your advice or your connection when you introduce people became something. I know that there are a lot of people who without their help I wouldn't be where I am, and I'd like to think I could do the same for others. I make a point to, if there's someone who is reaching out for information, I do my absolute best to share with them everything I've been taught.

Bonnie: How did you get your manager?

Dylan: I did a feature film called *Grave Encounters 2*. It was my first feature. They repped the directors, and they saw that film, and they contacted my agent and said, "If Dylan's not repped by an American manager, we'd love the opportunity." That was cool because at that point in my career I was just happy to have been on a film set. Then LA comes calling, right?

Bonnie: "Hello, LA? Yes, I'll take your calls."

Dylan: "Yes, I am available. Funny you should ask." That was Mystery Entertainment, and they asked if I wanted to be a part of the team, and I said yeah, and it's been good so far.

Bonnie: That's wonderful. I love these stories because again, it just illustrates that there's every different way to do this.

Dylan: And there's no one right way. I think the more people find out about their inspirations, the more they see there isn't one way. There are actors who went to UCLA. There are people who come over from England. They are kids plucked out of the Deep South, but the common thing that every one of them has is this belief that it's what they want to do and this understanding of, "I'd do it regardless of fame and money." If you enjoy what you're doing and you practice at it and you do well, people see that. They see the skill, and they see the passion, and they want to be around it. They want to be a part of it. I think that's the common undercurrent among all artists.

Bonnie: All successful artists.

Dylan: Yes. All successful artists. Exactly.

Brenna D'Amico

Brenna: One day I said, "Mom, I really want to do something more." I did Fox Valley Repertoire, which had a bit bigger of a musical theater production, and I love that, but I thought, "I want to get a manager or an agent," and she said okay. So we sent my headshot into this manager, and I auditioned for them, and they took me on.

I'm so grateful that they did that for me, and from there on out, that's what sort of kick-started where I am now. They got me my agent in LA, so I was really, really excited, because I was taping, just taping for a year until I got *Descendants*. I got *Descendants* my first week I was out there.

Which is really funny. I was only in LA for a week, but then I got a callback for the thing I went out there for... which then gave me the opportunity to audition for *Descendants*.

Bonnie: Okay, so let me back up so I can follow the trail here, because this is the thing that is among the hardest for new actors of any age frankly, not just young people: to get an agent or a manager and then to open that door. Once you walk through it, if you've got the talent and if you're what they're looking for, things often can go well, but just to get a meeting is so tough. So you were successful sending in a headshot and a résumé to the Chicago manager, who signed you.

Did you have an agent in Chicago?

Brenna: No, I didn't. I had an agent in LA, and that's where they got me. I actually did, after I got my agent in LA, have an agent in Chicago for a short amount of time for local things, but mostly my auditions were coming in from California.

Bonnie: Because that's where almost all the casting is.

Brenna: Yeah, that's where almost all the casting happens...It was so cool taping, but when I went in the room, that's when I really fell in love with this.

It's just such a different vibe, and I love it. That's what I prefer. I think that's what most actors prefer. Because you're one-on-one with them, you can really focus, and I love it. I love doing it.

Bonnie: You can feed off of each other's energy. You can feel the temperature of the room.

In the state of California and in New York, you really want to have an agent before a manager, because in those two states, managers are not allowed by law to get work for actors; only agents are. This is because agents are licensed and bonded, and managers are not. But you are from Chicago, so you were able to get a manager who could do stuff for you—get you work, get you set up.

Brenna: Exactly, so I was lucky. I was so lucky that that happened for me.

Bonnie: That's big. I like people to know that, because if you're not in California or New York, your path to a great agent might be through first signing with a manager. Once you've got one of those pieces in place, it's so much easier to have them set you up with a meeting.

Brenna: Exactly. It just kind of falls into place once you get that start that you're looking for. Even if it's really hard for you to find an agent or manager, there's so many things that can help you up your game. If you sing, you can post on social media, and that can help you.

There's just so many different ways. Take acting classes. There's so many ways to help you get the experience you need in order to get somebody, like managers or agents, interested.

Bonnie: Exactly, and people can't hear that enough I think, because there's a lot of, "I don't know how to do this." There's every different way to do this.

Brenna: So many different ways. There's musical theater. When you come in with a résumé with that experience, that can interest them. My résumé was filled with so many different plays that that kind of spiked their interest a bit.

Bonnie: If you're a good agent or manager, you can learn a lot just looking at a résumé, that a person outside the industry wouldn't even be able to intuit. So your manager gets you an appointment in LA with a prospective agent, or you were sent out for an audition?

Brenna: He visited Chicago and was scouting for new clients at my manager's office.

Bonnie: Then you flew out to LA for an audition?

Brenna: Yes, and it was my first time being in the room for a totally different one, not *Descendants*, and I got a call-back for that other one and had to stay another week. That's when he said, "Wait, I think I have another audition for you, and I'm gonna get you in." That was *Descendants*.

Bonnie: So you have the manager in Chicago. They get you out here for some auditions. How did you end up signing with Pamela Fisher at Abrams?

Brenna: I ended up signing with Pam because my manager and agent at the time, I separated from them. My lawyer actually referred us to Pam, for which I was really, really happy. I went in, and I knew that they were right for me. I knew that I wanted to be with them.

They were so amazing, and Domina and Pam are just...I love being with them, and I'm so grateful that I'm with them.

Joey Bragg

Joey: It's another thing that fell into my lap. I was doing stand-up for three years at this point, and I was almost sixteen. I did a bunch of shows in LA at the Hollywood Improv and Laugh Factory, and my second show ever was at the West Side Comedy Theater. The woman that was in my same management company that I'm still with—her name is Sarah Klegman—saw me and just saw something I guess, or saw an opportunity.

Bonnie: It's what they do. It's what their gift is, in part.

Joey: I met her, and I loved her. She's the sweetest lady. She's no longer a manager, but we're still friends. I met my then agent, who was a stand-up agent from ICM.

Bonnie: You started with the manager who found you at the comedy club; then did she set up a meeting with prospective agents?

Joey: That agent was also at that same show.

Bonnie: You got both the agent and the manager out of one show?

Joey: Out of one show, yeah.

            The agent was there to see me. The manager was there to see someone else. The manager just saw me perform, but the agent was there to see me perform.

Bonnie: That's amazing. Your story illustrates that there are a zillion ways up this mountain. There isn't just one way.

Joey: There's star power, or whatever that is, or the "It" factor, or the X factor, whatever you want to call it, but I think it's relative. If you want to be a writer and performer, start making YouTube videos, and just throw every idea you have out there. If you want to be a stand-up, go out there, and do it. If you want to be an actor, enlist in musical theater in your school and just do everything you can, because moving down here and hoping that somebody's going to see you and go, "You have the 'It' factor," is a crapshoot.

4

Training

ASK A ROOMFUL of actors whether training has been important to them, and you will get a full range of answers. Most will say absolutely yes, and a few will say no. However, the few who are self-taught will generally agree that their classroom was the stage, or the studio, or the many audition rooms in between.

These young actors are no exception. Cameron Boyce, Dove Cameron, and Joey Bragg fall into the "Learning by doing" camp. Thomas Doherty is conservatory trained. Booboo Stewart, Dylan Playfair, Garrett Clayton, Luke Benward, Jessica Marie Garcia, Sarah Jeffery, Brenna D'Amico, and Victoria Moroles all credit their training with giving them a big leg up on their success.

Whatever their own experience, every one of these actors agrees that the important thing is to find what works for you—and to do that.

Booboo Stewart

Booboo: I love training. I mean I love it, and I hate it. We have a love-hate relationship. Sometimes you just don't want to train. Sometimes you have the bug to train. No matter what your training is, whether you're training to be a dancer, an actor, or whatever…having that mental strength to be able to train…I think 50 percent of the battle is just to get yourself in there to train.

It's hard enough. I take my hat off to anyone who trains. Showing up prepared for whatever your job is. Not even an industry job. Whatever it is. I respect that.

Bonnie: When you're talking about training, you're talking about all kinds, aren't you? You're talking about dance training and weight training and martial arts training.

Booboo: Yep. All kinds of training. Acting. Even if your training is showing up and knowing all of your lines. I've worked with so many actors. They think that the work is getting the job. But it's not. I dislike auditioning so much, but unfortunately, that's…that's where my fun begins. After I get the job. The work is my audition, but I have fun on set. Everyone thinks that, "Oh, I got the job now. Woo! Yay! I can celebrate and have a good time." No, it's just starting.

The one I just did in the arctic, that was really intense. It was just very emotional up there. It's crazy. Working with an amazing scene partner, and an amazing cast, is so important. I think you could have someone who has never acted before in their life work with a great scene partner, and they would have a great performance. When you're not acting for yourself, that's when true emotions and honesty come out, I think. You can tell when some-one's acting for themselves. I think. I don't like it. That's such a selfish actor. You know what I mean?

Of course, I hate it when people say that theater is for acting or for actors and cinema isn't. That's so untrue. I think it has to be more. Cinema has to be for acting and actors because you have to do it so many times in a row, and you have to be there every single day for hours and hours, and it's such an interesting thing.

Bonnie: I'm so happy you brought that up because, you know, a lot of actors who end up in TV and film come from a theater background. There's an assumption in the culture that "real acting" occurs on the stage.

Booboo: It's all real acting. I've never done stage acting, but I'm assuming when you're on stage, you're so immersed, and so it's easier to get out because you're literally surrounded by it and you're going from the start to finish. When you're acting on set, you have to create it. It has to come from a certain place. Actors, I think, have to be more of a family.

Bonnie: Acting in TV and film, you are interrupted constantly. And there's no arc. You have to create the arc ongoingly.

Booboo: Just constantly. Yeah, someone's moving a light. "Ah, darn it." In your head you're like "I don't want to stop the scene but..." Yes, it's different. It's interesting.

Dove Cameron

Dove: I get pretty divided on this because I have seen a lot of people change the way that they approach their craft— I hate that word; it's so pretentious—their "craft." They change their level of involvement, finesse, talent—I don't know—with acting class and voice lessons. I have talked to enough people where I have been bold enough to say, "It doesn't matter. Do whatever you want. Who cares—you're born with it." I've spoken to enough actors who would just slam me down for that and insist, "You don't understand what it did for me." Now I can recognize and see what a difference it can make for a lot of people.

I am not the kind of person who works well in a class environment. I took a couple of acting classes, and I was…I'm not ADHD, but I'm something, and so I definitely felt, "All right, I want to absorb ten classes in one class, and this is moving too slow for me. I have to wait around, and I don't like this, and I want to jump up and down and learn really quickly. I want to learn at my own pace," so I peaced-out pretty quick. I basically just sat at home and watched movie after movie and studied the people that I respected.

That's not for everybody. I do think that's an individual thing. I think you should try a couple of classes with some well-respected acting teachers. You know, look it up first, because there can be a lot of sketchy people, but look up who's well respected. Look up the teachers that agents like, and that may take a little digging, but it's definitely easy to find via a couple of Google clicks.

In terms of voice lessons, I do think they are always helpful. People who I know now who have been singing and working for forty years in this industry still take voice lessons. Kristin Chenoweth takes voice lessons. Anybody can and should, I think, take voice lessons, if not just to protect your voice. I have to do that. I speak a lot, I speak very loudly, I kind of never shut up, and I sing a lot too.

I sing as often as I speak. I always think "I can hit that high note without warming up and without supporting it. No problem. Eight times in a row? Let's do it." I definitely have to take voice lessons just to not ruin myself.

Dylan Playfair

Dylan: For me, training was really important because when I'm in a class with other people, I can't turn off the observation. Every single human being doing a scene to me is information that you can use.

I think every actor is different. I know a lot of actors who swear by not training, who have a feeling for their process that they're really comfortable with, and then I meet actors who are convinced that if you don't go to England for five years, you're a phony. So, I think there's a really broad spectrum in there, and you've got to find what works for you. What worked for me was getting out of my body. Coming from an athletic background, I was really stuck in my physicality. I was really having a hard time emoting. I was doing a lot of things that a lot of athletes do when they try to perform.

For me, having someone watch and critique me was something I was used to from being coached. It was something I wanted. I really wanted that structure. I wanted to know what the work looked like. I didn't have an idea of what acting homework was. I just saw people on TV and thought, "How do you practice that?"

I started learning tools, like breaking down scripts and understanding objectives and listening to your partner and breaking down the subtext and things that I would've probably not learned for a long time down the road on set, which all really counted. Then there were the perspectives to me that didn't work. Because I knew they didn't work, they were valuable. I think that's another thing that people lose sight of...learning how to not do it can be just as valuable as learning how to do it.

Bonnie: I love that. I just got how coming from an athletic background and being used to the idea of being coached, understanding the value of a coach, and what that means for you just directly translates into acting. Why would you fight that?

Dylan: It did. For me, it was something that if I didn't take the time to go coach and practice and learn, I didn't feel that I was working at it. I needed to feel that I was learning something. What that's done for me is it's made me feel really good about the success that's come because I don't feel that I stumbled into anything. If there ever was a conversation where God forbid I would ever have to defend my success, if there ever comes that day where someone says it's overnight, I can say, "No, man, I've sat on sets for twenty-two hours watching generators. I've sat in class in hot casting director workshops where my scene is two minutes long and they say, 'That was really good. Thanks.' Come on, teach me something."

I've gone through a lot of these things, and I think I have a respect for it now. I don't know if I would have had that same amount of respect for the job had I come into it and right away booked something big.

Garrett Clayton

Garrett: I've never technically stopped training. Even leaving high school, I went to the BFA program, and then when I left, I came out here.

In LA, I initially went to Warner Loughlin for about six months, and I loved it there. I thought their process was fascinating because in the program I was in, I was learning Alexander technique, and this one was different. Then I went to Lesly Kahn for about a year. I've studied with Catherine Carlen, who also goes to the Actors' Studio and teaches there sometimes, as well as studies there, because the Actors' Studio is wonderful. Bob Garrett, as well, I've studied with, and he's worked with incredible people. Anyone who knows Bob knows he's worked with really wonderful people, like Hugh Jackman, Drew Barrymore, Jessica Lange, you name it.

I have three vocal coaches. I have three acting coaches. Because I think you can learn so many different things from different people.

Bonnie: I totally agree. As someone who really values loyalty—I'm an extremely loyal person; at the same time, when it comes to coaches and teachers, everybody has something different to teach you—I think it's kind of crazy to just pigeonhole yourself with one person.

Garrett: I don't know if people hear it often outside of the city, but you need to learn what works for you. Different techniques and different teachers and coaches just have different skill sets and can teach you different ways to approach material.

I mean, even right now, I'm always simultaneously study-ing with different people...I don't know if I'm a masochist or I just want to be exhausted all the time.

Gregory Berg simultaneously teaches at Yale part of the year, so I've been trying to study with the Yale technique. It's just fascinating the different ways you can approach material. I applaud someone who can just show up to set and fully flesh out a character without ever studying, but I can't, and I don't know a lot of people who would want to.

Bonnie: Most actors want training.

Garrett: As well as different ways to approach things. I mean... I've gotten characters who were supposed to have been raised in a forest. Catherine, who I mentioned earlier, she had a very fascinating way of approaching it. She said, "I want you to find a dark space." She goes, "Go sit in your closet..." because when you can turn off one of your senses, they always say everything else is heightened, but nobody tells you to actually go do it.

She said, "I want you to go in there, and I want you to just start really feeling the texture of things and trying to see if there's anything you've never smelled before." I mean, whether it's good or bad, because it's a closet— there's shoes.

"Can you hear anything? Can you hear the neighbors? Can you hear people in the next room, and how close and far away are they?" So...when I am this character, now I can approach it from an animalistic point of view, because if you're surviving in the woods, you're surviving off your instincts. I wouldn't have thought to do that.

Most people would just start writing down "I ams" or "I believe in" or "This is my history," but how are you going to approach it physically? How are you going to be comfortable in the body of that human being?

Bonnie: Which is what conveys so much of the character.

Garrett: Yeah.

Cameron Boyce

Cameron: My training is very different than other people's training. I've never really actually taken an acting class, and I think people are very shocked by that. A lot of people really benefit from acting class, and I'm sure I would take a lot of things from acting class as well. I think as an actor, you have to really go to a certain place. I feel like if I try to constantly be in that place, I'll wear myself out almost.

My training is really, if I'm running lines for an audition that I have or something like that, I will run the lines enough to be really familiar with them. I will really think about the words, because everything has a purpose on the page. Every single thing on the page is there for a reason. It's like in the Declaration of Independence, where literally every single word down to the "the" is there for a reason. It could be replaced with another word and give that sentence a completely different meaning, right?

Everything on the page is there for a reason, and you have to think, why is it there? Why does the writer want this specific thing in the script? Once you break it down like that, then you have a better understanding of where you want to take it.

A lot of people see words, and they say words. You can do that. I've seen that in shows and movies, and they're never talked about as being good performances. Sometimes, miraculously they make it for whatever reason, but when you really break it down, when you break a script down or sides down or whatever, once you understand that every single thing on the page is there to convey something, is there to explain something to the audience, then you really can go line for line and a lot of times word for word.

That's something that I really look at. When I have the understanding and I'm familiar with the words and I feel comfortable, I put it down. I put it down, and I look at it right before I go in, and I get myself back into that place. When people run things over and over again...and sometimes it works for people, if that's your method, then it's cool. But for me, things get stale, and they just dry up, and there's nothing natural about it anymore. When you go in knowing this is exactly how I want to say this line, that never happens.

There's nothing natural about that anymore. Me talking to you right now, I'm not thinking in my head, "This is how I'm going to say whatever I'm about to say to Bonnie." That doesn't happen in real life. Once you take it there, it becomes robotic. For me, I like to understand why. I like to understand whatever feeling I want to have in the certain moment. I do want to know that, but I don't want to know down to the last bit how I'm going to say something or how this is going to be read. That's never good.

What I do is I get really familiar with it beforehand. You do work before, and then once you've done the work, there's really nothing to fear anymore. When you've done the work, there's nothing that you have to worry about. You'll leave it at the door, and then you let the work speak for itself, and you just go to the place naturally. That's just how it should be, I feel like.

Bonnie: You were fortunate enough, unlike the vast majority of actors out there, to be able to be in a position to learn by doing with some of the best. But not everybody has that incredible fortune. I think for those people, that's where acting classes can really close that gap.

Cameron: Right, it's important. I'm so lucky, because like I said before, I was literally in it before I knew I was in it. People always ask me, "So, Cameron, you've just graduated high school. Are you going to go to college?" I tell them, I've already been to college. I've already taken courses. I've toyed around with really expensive cameras, and I've talked to grips, and I've talked to FX people. I've literally been where people train to be in college. If I went and did film or whatever at USC, that's a great program, and I'm sure I would learn a lot, but I've learned enough just being in it, being around it. I'm literally on set.

A lot of people really take that for granted when they're on set. They don't ask questions.

You have an opportunity to really learn. One thing that I've noticed is that first of all, actors don't, a lot of the time, ask questions about what a grip does or whoever it is. When an actor does ask, that grip is going to be like, "Wait, really? Okay, I'll tell you everything." They're so ready to pass their knowledge on. I've always felt like an actor is in a prime position to learn about anything, because when you're on set, maybe you're not in a scene. You're not really needed anywhere, so you can just roam and ask questions and start to really break other jobs down because a lot of people aren't actors for the rest of their careers.

You see, so many actors go from actor to producer to director to whatever, right? It's never, "I'm just an actor." Every really great actor has also done stuff behind the camera.

Bonnie: They've been producing; they've been writing or directing.

Cameron: Absolutely. In their free time, they're toying with things, and they're playing around. That's something that I've noticed, and that's what I want. That's the path that I want to go down. I don't want to be one-dimensional. I want to be well rounded, and I want to not only know what's happening, but that also makes the respect for other people on set so much greater. Once people start respecting each other on set and start to really throw ideas around, and if an actor understands what a certain guy does on set, then there's a mutual respect that is really a bonding. It builds camaraderie, and it just makes everything better. It makes everything run smoothly.

There's really no downside to that. Just ask questions. Even if you're in acting class or you're wherever, just ask the questions anyway. You don't have to be on set to learn, because I don't know everything. Nobody really knows everything, but wherever it is that you are, if you're in acting class or you're in theater camp or wherever, just ask questions and try to understand where the other person is coming from, because that really not only benefits you, but it benefits them. It's a whole cycle.

Bonnie: Just like you said about a script, there's a reason for every word on the page.

Cameron: There's a reason for everyone on set.

Bonnie: Why they're there and why they're doing what they're doing the way they're doing it, there's always a reason. You may not understand it, but you'll probably do better when you do.

Cameron: For example, and this is so simple: There's a guy on set whose designated job is to make sure that the camera is in focus. What they do is they take a tape measure and they put the base of the tape measure right by the lens, and then they take the tape measure and they put it really close to your face. Because I understand now what that guy does, I just take the tape measure in my hand and I put it right to my eye. They always go, "Thanks, man." It's just so simple, but there's just something there, and there's a respect there now. I probably helped him. He probably wouldn't have got it close to my face, because he would've been scared to hit me. I take the tape measure, I put it right to my eye, so the focus should be perfect, and we get a better shot. And I am building relationships.

Luke Benward

Luke: My mom taught me everything I know. I've done some classes here and there. I haven't really enjoyed or seen a need for scene studies. I've been involved, and I really tried to immerse myself, and I've had some really good partners and really great scenes that I think have helped me.

I have a problem, I think, paying for someone's opinion. I know when I'm really invested in the moment. I've been doing it long enough that I know when I'm in the moment. For me to be there, to really get it out and know that I hit the mark and to be told that I didn't and then to be told by my peers that it was incredible and that I did…it's not constructive criticism if you're trying to get me to come back and be in your class again. That was what it felt like.

That's kind of my main thing with classes, but my mom taught me everything I know. It was me and her growing up. We did all my tapes, and she's helped other actors and actresses who've come out of Nashville. You know, Miley and…

Bonnie: That's Miley Cyrus for anybody who's curious…

Luke: Miley Cyrus, yeah. Actually, another of her former students is on *Stranger Things* right now. Natalia Dyer. She plays the older sister of one of the young kids.

Yeah, there've been a few. She did that. Growing up, we had a nice wall in the kitchen that we always used.

Bonnie: To shoot audition tapes?

Luke: Audition tapes and audition tapes and audition tapes, yeah. We made tons. She definitely did it enough years to kind of figure out how to convey emotion—how to bring someone to their honest self. It's really cool. She has a gift for it, without a doubt.

Bonnie: She does. You had the great good fortune of having a mom who was already an actress and an acting coach and a very fine one. And let's be honest, not every actor is going to be a good acting coach.

Luke: Uh-huh. It takes an honesty that is quite rare, really, to convey your emotions and to bring emotions out of people.

Jessica Marie Garcia

Jessica: There are a lot of people that never had an acting class and never had a problem, but for me, it wasn't as much about learning how to act. That's a different thing. It's being able to be vulnerable enough to become a different human and find out other people's human traits and not judge other people's human traits because you can't…Once I was able to break that wall down and be an actor who's fearless and be able to do *Who's Afraid of Virginia Woolf*—I did that play for a long time—and I was coming home at night for a month thinking, why am I so depressed?

I'm in such a dark place, and I realized, "Of course, because I'm losing a made-up child. I'm losing my son every night on stage. Of course, I'm going to feel this way. My teacher really helped me to learn where to put that, more so, than to become an actor. It was really how to still have Jessica when you're becoming all these different people, because it made sense why people take pills and do things to try and mellow themselves out because you're literally—I was losing a son and then I did a scene where I had just lost my husband—you bring out these dark things, and you need to be able to shut that off and leave that.

Bonnie: Close the door; put it away. It's so important, and a lot of actors are really confused by that.

Jessica: Of course.

Sarah Jeffery

Sarah: I think it differs from person to person. Training can be super important or it can be not as important for some people. I definitely recommend at least giving it a go and seeing where it gets you. I started training a little bit when I was younger with the dancing. It was less serious, but it was some good background training, and getting over the nerves almost, because that can be a part of it for some people.

Getting comfortable using your voice in front of people, and being in front of the camera, that was a big part of training for me. I've done a few intensives here and there, and I think it's very useful to pick what works for you and what doesn't, try people's techniques. It definitely doesn't mean that it's going to work for you 100 percent, but for me it's important to at least to give it a go.

Bonnie: I think if you find the right teacher or the right school that really resonates with the way you operate, that can be really wonderful, and you are probably not going to find that on the first go. Maybe you try an acting class, and you think, "I'm not getting anything out of this." That doesn't mean you should never try another acting class again. Try a different teacher; try a different school.

Sarah: The odds are very low that you will find that perfect fit the first time. Additionally, for me, my dad has been a huge part of training and getting comfortable. That's one of the biggest things I'm grateful for in terms of my career—is having my dad to guide me and help me and be honest with me, because that's a huge thing. When I'm a little torn, if I'm giving the right delivery, or some-thing doesn't feel right, he will always be honest with me.

Bonnie: That's so beautiful. I think, in general, in life, whether we're talking about actors or whatever, that parents really do their kids a disservice by saying that every sin-gle thing that they do is wonderful all the time. How can you do better and improve and become really who you might become in the world if you don't get some honest feedback? What a gift that is.

Sarah: Such a gift. Sometimes we get frustrated with one another, but it's been a huge source of help for me through all of this and to also already have a great rela-tionship with my dad and be comfortable with him, it's been a blessing.

Joey Bragg

Joey: I have an acting coach that I go to for certain auditions, and I feel like I've learned a lot from him, but I haven't been in an acting class.

I think acting is one of those things where there's a difference between people that are classically trained, and people that are just learning from doing, but I also think that I don't ever feel like I'm very good at it. I feel like I trust my opinion of what I think I should be doing, but there's no part of me that thinks I'm better than the other people that are going out for my thing.

When I go to an audition, my mind-set isn't, "I'm gonna blow them away with my reading." My mind-set is, "I'm going to introduce myself and be personable, and they're going to like Joey and then think, 'Oh, I like Joey enough to have him be the character,' rather than, 'I like Joey's portrayal of the character.'"

Bonnie: That's so funny.

Joey: Yeah. There's so many things that I want to be doing that I'm not doing, and it's not because I can't do them. It's just laziness. I mean, I want to be going to stand-up shows every night and doing that. I want to be writing more, but then, when an audition comes, I do that. Balancing is a hard thing in this business.

Bonnie: It is. And your schedule's so unpredictable because it's completely at the effect of whatever shows up in your inbox late at night or first thing in the morning. It's like, "Oh, I was going to do this today, but now I'm going to do that. I was going to go to the dentist, or I was going to go write my thing for the stand-up, but now I'm going to run a bunch of sides and go drive across town."

Joey: Yeah, exactly. And so I always end up trying to balance everything. I feel constantly like I'm not doing enough, but I think that that's the only way. To do what you want to do is to feel like you're never doing enough.

Brenna D'Amico

Brenna: Training is so important. You can never learn or know too much about what you love. I go to acting class at Lisa Picotte's Acting Studio once a week. I love it there. We do comedy; we do drama. What I need to work on most is my comedy. I can't get enough of that, because challenges are what excite me. Challenges are what people need, and I think if you kind of just stay where you're comfortable, that's not going to give you as much success as you deserve.

I think those challenges are so important for you to take on and realize how special and important they are to you and for you. I also do singing lessons, and I'm really excited because learning so many new things about my voice recently is super exciting for me. I get in my head a lot; I really do. Just the fact that my teacher has opened this new door to what my voice can do, I'm really excited to play around with the high notes that I just realized that I can sing from now on.

Bonnie: Singing is really powerful, and getting on top of that can be so empowering for the human that you are, not just for the performer that you are.

I think it's that metaphor that we use about finding your voice. There's something there. When you really do find your voice, when you can speak your truth, there's something incredibly liberating about that.

Voice lessons, even for singing, seem to unlock that for a lot of people.

Brenna: I agree. It's really freeing, having somebody show you something that you thought you couldn't do and learning...I love being in acting class, because there's so many amazing actors that I can learn from...because there's no one way with doing anything, ever. Just being able to experience so many different ways, I think is quite beautiful.

Bonnie: I do too. I'm just one of those lifelong learners, but I've always been inspired by seeing what other people do and how they do it. Maybe once I check something out, it's not going to be for me, but I'll still learn something.

There's always something you can take away. There's always something you can do to become better at what you do, and if you really love something, why wouldn't you always want to get better at it?

Brenna: Exactly. I love that, what you just said. Why wouldn't you want to get better at it? Like, "Oh, I've taken a month of acting class. I know everything there is to know." That is not the case. You can never learn too much about what you love.

Bonnie: I agree. At the same time, there are different ways to learn. I'm a reader. Books and the written word, that's how I take in information. Other people, they just don't really read, and they learn better by watching or by doing. You know, if you learn best by doing, you don't necessarily learn much by taking a class. Sometimes you learn a lot in the audition process. Over and over again, all the auditions you guys have to go through. That's it's own school in some ways.

Brenna: It is, and it's great to go in there and learn what differ-ent casting directors want, and kind of being able to read them a little bit, and so many people get really discour-aged about hearing the word "no," because you are going to hear the word "no" more than the word "yes" so many times. What I do is I let that motivate me to get that "yes," to hear that "yes," and to want that "yes" even more.

Bonnie: I love that. It's true. Think about it: however many people audition for any given role, all of them are going to hear no, except for one person.

Brenna: Yeah, all of them except for that one person. That should just motivate you even more to be that one person.

Thomas Doherty

Thomas: I think training has been amazing. It's been fantastic. It kind of sets you up for this discipline in the industry. I think the vigorous dance training and just the whole dis-cipline that goes along with all of that has been fantastic for such an intense industry as well. At the same time, I think training can be a hindrance. I think it pumps a lot of fear into you.

I think with training, because you're in such a confined space with the same people for three or four years, and the goal's always the same, but no one knows what the goal is; it's this kind of notion of what you want to achieve or become. Because there's no real evidence of what that is, there's that buildup of almost anxiety. And you need to get an agent, that's one big thing. Everyone around you, your peers, people that are similar to you, they all want an agent. When that's so concentrated for a number of years, this delusion starts to build up. Then that competitiveness builds up.

When you've got so much competitiveness and so much delusion and so much anxiety, it starts to outweigh the creativity and the balance of why you actually did it in the first place. I noticed that myself. When I got an agent I was like, "Right, I need to get a job." I got my job and without even enjoying the job I was like, "Right, I need to get...When's my next job? When's my next job going to be?" I got my next job. When's my next job going to be? It just zaps away the reason you started doing it in the first place.

Bonnie: Sounds like you're talking specifically about the model of conservatory training.

Thomas: Yeah, and I go back to London, and my friends have all just graduated, and that fear in their voices and in their minds, in what they're saying, I was no exception, like I just said. It's that instead of the craft being the main focus, people get caught up in the industry—in the peripheral stuff, in the egotistical stuff. Then you get sucked into this thing that you didn't want in the first place.

Bonnie: It's got nothing to do with the art, really.

Thomas: Nothing to do with the art, yeah. When you kind of bring yourself out of that, you see it, and it's like, "Oh no! This is so sad, because this isn't why we all did this in the first place." You see people, and they lose their spark, and it then starts to become fame driven and financially driven. It's such a sacred industry outside of the world of finance and for creativity.

Bonnie: People don't talk about this. So many actors or performers, they enter into the business because they're in love with the art of it. It makes them feel alive. If you lose your balance and get too much about the externals instead of the internals, then you start getting driven by things outside of you, which is inherently toxic. I think that's what you're talking about.

Thomas: Yeah, absolutely. I found that even in college. I remember being confused, because here we were, we wanted to create something new. We wanted to be in this creative space and bounce off of each other, and inspire each other, and be inspired to do different things, obscure things. Just test the waters, try things. Then I found myself in this situation where you were scared to sing, because people were judging you. Then no one wanted to express themselves because of fear of failure, I guess. Fear of failure.

I can't speak for America. I don't know if it's any different out here, but definitely in Britain, that's the case. These schools can be...not my ex-school; MGA Academy was actually a nice school. There were elements of it. But these big London schools, you spend thousands and thousands and thousands of pounds, and it's just this toxic atmosphere that defeats the purpose of what you're trying to achieve.

It's so ironic and sad, and when you're so young as well, you're so fragile, your mind. I mean I still really am, but at seventeen you're so influenced. I don't think you've created a solid sense of self yet, so you're easily swayed. You're easily roped into that negative spiral, that counterproductive spiral.

Bonnie: I've seen you dance, and the level of ability you have, for example, specifically with dance...could you have had that without your training?

Thomas: Yeah, you can, you can, absolutely. Self-training. There's so many classes. All different styles.

What I mean is...you don't need to go to an institute, and you don't need to spend thousands and thousands of pounds a year to do that. You can be very savvy, and it might require a little bit more work. I mean it's kind of like you go...it's like an all-inclusive holiday. You pay this money, and then it's an all-inclusive, you get to eat what you want, whereas self-training is like going inter-railing in Europe. You've got to find your own way.

Bonnie: Totally doable though.

Thomas: Totally doable. As well, you stumble upon things that you would never have gotten in this all-inclusive holiday. As a creative person, and as an actor and dancer or singer, you want more exposure. You want different things. The more exposure to different things you can get, the better you're going to be. The more experience you have, the better you're going to be. So all-inclusive holidays are fantastic. But I think it's important for people to know that they can do it on their own. I never did it on my own, but I know some incredible, incredible performers that did it on their own. There's a purity to it as well, because they're not in that toxic environment.

Bonnie: Yes, so there's every different way to do it.

Thomas: The more I'm thinking about it, the more we're talking about it, you do not need to go to a school. You do not need that. There are copious amounts of classes and lectures, if you'd even call them that, out there. Especially in LA.

Bonnie: Well, there are acting schools all over the place here. But when we say acting schools in LA, it's not generally like a two- or three-year conservatory program. You just sign up for classes.

Thomas: Honestly, I think that is actually quite a good way to do it. I really do, because you're not regimented in this. You're a creative person, and you can't regiment a creative person. If you do, then you just sap the life out of it.

Bonnie: Yes, take a voice class here, take an Improv class there. Go for what excites you, and maybe what you need some support in.

Thomas: Absolutely. That's the thing: always, always, always work on your weaknesses, because you become a more rounded, wholesome performer.

Victoria Moroles

Victoria: I think training has been very important for me. I don't train as much as I used to when I first got out here. I was taking a lot of acting classes and also doing school, and that was hard to balance. I was auditioning, doing classes and then school. I felt like it was really important. I feel now that it just depends on what kind of person you are, or what kind of artist you are. I think that it helped me figure out how to work at my craft every day, because we have a very inconsistent job.

Unless you are at work every day, you are not normally doing anything or working on something for an audition. Say you have no auditions, no work. You need to still be progressing. I felt like classes really did that for me. I dabbled around, it's not that you don't click with different teachers. It's like you can click with somebody but then also going to somebody else, you can get different things from them and pull from whatever you like and what connects to you.

Bonnie: I'm a really big believer in that. I think it's special, and it's wonderful and exciting when you can find a teacher or school or a class that you really get a lot of value from and you really resonate with. At the same time, if you stay with them and only them, you are missing out on all kinds of other approaches that you don't know are out there, and you are not going to become the kind of well-rounded artist that you might be.

Victoria: Right, and you can always go back to them. I started out going to an ongoing class with Dan Savell, and I loved Emmis; he's great. I totally connected with him. Then I went to Margie Haber, and then I found Zak Barnett, and I love Zak. I studied with him for a couple of years. Now he's just, I feel like kind of more my mentor. I can just call him if I ever needed anything.

I did intensives, Improv. I think it's really beneficial. You can always go try a class, and if you don't like it, don't go. I know a lot of actors who just don't like going to class or they don't want a coach, or they just do their own thing. That's awesome too. You kind of find a balance. I have found a balance, I don't go to class every week now unless I just want to drop in or something, but it definitely benefited me when I first started out. That's for sure.

Bonnie: I think people have different styles of learning, and they have different things that work for them, and the trick is to find what works for you and to do it.

Victoria: Exactly.

5

School

SCHOOL CAN BE a wonderful experience or an awful experience, and for many young people it's both. Young actors have the extra issue of balancing auditions and work on top of their studies, and this challenge on top of the regular challenges can lead many of them to try different approaches to getting an education.

Kids who are artists sometimes feel different from their peers. They don't always have the same interests as many kids of their own age, which can make them feel "weird." Some of these kids have an easier time talking to and working with adults than kids their own age. Even if they feel like they fit in easily, the experience of leaving school for chunks of time to work can create a sense of separation, both socially and academically.

Many young actors end up on some kind of alternative educational path—attending homeschool, online school, special schools for professional kids, or on-set tutoring. Some finish school early.

The choices are not always easy. But as you'll see on the following pages, each of these young actors found their way through school on their own terms...sometimes with a little creativity, and usually with a lot of hard work.

Cameron Boyce

Cameron: I stayed in public school until sixth grade. That was hard. I would get a Burger King commercial. I'd be gone for two days, and I'd come back to school, and I didn't know what was happening. I had no idea what was happening in math or English or anything like that.

Bonnie: You missed that important day where you're learning a central concept about the math, and the rest of the year is confusing for you.

Cameron: Completely. Studio teachers have a different way of teaching things. It was just hard. When I booked *Jessie* in 2011, I was going into the seventh grade. I went to home-schooling, which was very weird, and it didn't feel like real school. It still doesn't really feel like real school. I did work, I wrote in books, and I read books, and I did all that stuff from seventh until twelfth grade, but something about those years feels very like, I don't really think I was fully doing school. That's because there's so many other things that I had to think about.

It was like I had two jobs. I would literally go from being on set and being in the scene and being a character. Then once my scene was done, our first AD would say, "All right, Cameron, go to school." Then I would go to crafty, grab a soda, and then walk upstairs and go to school.

We would literally wait for our second AD to come upstairs and say, "Go to set," because we didn't want to be in school. We wanted to be on set the whole time, so we would just wait patiently in school to go back to set.

It was like a really long bathroom break in public school, like, "Can I go to the bathroom?" I got probably as good of an education as a kid in public school. I just think that with a one-on-one setting with a tutor, you probably understand things a little more, and they work a little harder to help you understand.

Public school moves really quickly, and there are thirty other kids that the teacher has to worry about. If you don't get it, sorry, we're moving on anyway, but with us, there were four kids and two teachers.

Bonnie: That's an incredible ratio.

Cameron: Yeah, and granted, we were in different grades, with different curriculums. At the same time, we had two teachers practically to ourselves.

Bonnie: You're just basically being private tutored to all the way through seventh to twelfth grade.

Cameron: Exactly. Really, as much as it was a disadvantage that I had to also work, it was also totally an advantage to have a teacher who really cared about what it was that I was doing. That was really helpful. Kids who go to regular school don't always have to worry about other things like I did. But a lot of time, they do. They're doing sports and whatever. They're doing their thing. I had a job, and I had school, and I got through both pretty well, I'd like to think. Yeah, it was tough, but you get through it. With that kind of support, it's hard to fail. Our teachers cared so much about how well we did in school, and I graduated with honors.

Bonnie: You went all the way through. You never took the CHSPE (California High School Proficiency Exam), because you didn't really have to. There was no reason.

Cameron: No. There really wasn't. I would've if I had to, but a lot of people take the CHSPE, and sometimes it works, and sometimes it doesn't. If you want to take the CHSPE because a casting director really likes you, but they might have to go with somebody older, because you're still in school and that costs production more money, and you can't be on the set for as long, then take the CHSPE. Totally take the CHSPE. I would've, but I was on set on a Disney show where there were other kids. We were all doing school. I think Karan didn't take the CHSPE. Peyton might've, but she graduated. And Skye's still in school, so that's just how we did it.

               I didn't want to cheat myself. It was already a fake experience…It wasn't really school anyway. That's what I'm all about, is staying normal as much as possible. I didn't want to cheat myself out of that. A lot of people in my graduating class didn't even go to graduation, because they're actors and they're too good for it or whatever, but I went with Karan and we had a blast. Sophie (Reynolds), we were all there. It's really nice to have that normal time. My grandparents came and it was the whole thing. That's really important. You learn to cherish that when your life is so abnormal.

Bonnie: It's really true. When things get super abnormal, the normal stuff becomes something you really do cherish and you look for, and it helps to keep you grounded literally.

For anybody who doesn't know what we're talking about, the CHSPE is the California High School Proficiency Exam. In California, young actors either at the end of their sophomore year or at sixteen can take this test. If they pass it, they get the equivalent of a high school diploma. They can be legally done with school. They don't have to have a set teacher anymore, and they can work adult hours, which is like the golden ticket.

Cameron: Yeah, you get these fifteen-, sixteen-year-olds who are on set all night and not doing school. I remember talking to a bunch of actors who were sixteen, and I'm thirteen or fourteen at the time. I'm asking them about their schooling, and they're saying, "I don't do school anymore."

I'm like, "What? How old are you? How are you out of school?" My first reaction to that was like, "Heck, yeah, I'm doing that," like any other kid. But once I got to that point I thought, "No, I'm not going to cheat my way out of it. Finish it."

Bonnie: I love hearing that, because I feel personally that the CHSPE is a very double-edged tool. It's not something anybody should do casually. It's not like if you take it, you have to be done with school. You can keep going to school all the way through and keep the certificate in your back pocket, but my experience is that when people do take it, they tend to use it.

They tend to not finish school, because they don't have to. Dove passed the CHSPE, and for her, it was the right thing. But to me, it's a very individual choice that has everything to do with you. The specific kid and the specific family and their specific career and where they're at. If you don't have to, don't do it.

Cameron: Yeah, as much as I talk about, "Oh well, I didn't really do school." I really was in school. And I got honors. I'm very proud of myself. But I think, when you're sixteen and you're done with school, you're missing out on two years of school. That's the math. That's the simple math.

You subtract eleventh and twelfth grade, and you learn a lot in those years.

Bonnie: Not to put too fine a point on it, but in fact, if you do finish school early because you passed the CHSPE, you're done with high school legally, but that doesn't mean you have the credits to get into college.

If you decided you want to do that, you have to work extra hard online or at a community college to be able to get into a college or university. Now, you may never decide to do that if your acting career takes off, but let's be honest; most actors' careers don't.

Cameron: It's so unstable. People say the CHSPE and a high school diploma are equivalent, because that's like the technical term for it, but people don't look at it the same way as a diploma. I say, do whatever is best for you. If it's better for you to not have to worry about school and you have a workload that's insane—we just attested to it with Dove; she was literally playing two characters—in that case, you take the CHSPE. That's the thing to do.

For me, I was very comfortable on set. I was fourth on the cast lists, so a lot of times I was in the B story, and I was chilling. There was no reason for me to. I'm so glad that I've finished school. It is normal, but that's still something to be proud of, and I'm very proud of it.

Victoria Moroles

Victoria: I went to middle school up until seventh grade in my hometown in Rockport, Texas, South Texas. I think I left in the middle of seventh grade. I was doing the whole thing. I was cheering, and I was really trying to stay in it and have that normal life back at home as much as I could, and then also come out here and do that for a while. In 2009, in February, we decided to just pick up, sell the house, and move...the whole thing. So after we fully moved out here, I just did online schooling.

And then I also did the Charter Options For Youth. It's a school for kids who can't go to school full time. I knew a lot of friends who were doing it. You go and then bring the work back home. You do it; then you go and test a couple of times a week. I did that for about a year or two, and then I took the CHSPE, and I studied really hard for that. I actually never fully graduated high school. I just took the CHSPE.

Do I look back and think I probably could have finished high school and graduated? Of course. But when you are around fifteen or sixteen in this industry, you are kind of pushed to be a legal eighteen because if you have somebody who is fifteen, but a legal eighteen, who can work longer hours versus somebody who is just fifteen, who needs a set teacher and can work fewer hours, the legal eighteen gets the job. It's crazy. I realized to make it really worth it, I'd need to be a legal eighteen.

Bonnie: If you are going to sacrifice so much that you are going to relocate and move out here so that you can go for it...I think of it as a kind of trough where all of a sudden, like you said, if you are fifteen, sixteen, seventeen, then you are competing with actors who are actually eighteen and older, who can play those same ages and work twelve hours a day.

Victoria: Like myself now.

Bonnie: Like you now, or kids who were in fact that age range, but they've passed the CHSPE and so they are a legal eighteen. When casting has that choice versus a kid who can only work six hours a day because they're a minor and have to put in three hours of school as well, it's kind of a no-brainer. You are not able to compete on a level playing field. There is huge pressure to do it, and it's a tough choice for a lot of families. There are real upsides and downsides. For a career, it can be a godsend.

Victoria: Exactly, and it was.

Bonnie: And it made a huge difference for us too. But then the downside is that really may be the end of your schooling. Are you going to be okay with that?

Victoria: I am. It did completely switch it around for me. I started to get a lot more auditions. Right after I had done that, I booked an episode at *CSI*, which they were only going to do legal eighteen for. It definitely was worth it. I think about it now, and I do want to go to college eventually. I do have some ambition to do something else.

And just knowing I have the option is really nice, because you miss out on all the high school stuff.

I feel like Disney was a really big high school experience for me. It's silly to think about it in that way but it was. I feel like I still got that.

Bonnie: I think Dove feels about the same way. *Liv and Maddie* felt like four years of high school. That was her four years. One group of people and special memories and coming of age.

Victoria: Proms.

Bonnie: Proms! They are pretty good about that stuff. Your school experience is actually very similar to a lot of actors. You experiment till you find what works, and you just kind of have to keep fine-tuning it: homeschooling, online, and Options, which is a kind of school for young professionals. A lot of actors, and sometimes athletes, go to those schools. Then you leave early to get your legal eighteen, so you can be a professional.

Victoria: A majority of my friends also took the CHSPE and still finished high school. That's wonderful. It's good that there is always an option with that and that the CHSPE just means that you can work longer hours. You can decide what you want to do. I think it just depends on whatever journey you think you are going to go on, because I didn't know back then. My mom was supportive enough to just let me do that and say, "Hey, I know that you can go to college later, but I think that you should do this on the way." I totally respect her for that, just for her to believe in me that much. God bless her.

Joey Bragg

Joey: School is such a different world. I wish I could go back and tell myself, "None of this matters. You're not going to remember any of these people's names come four years from now. Just absorb everything you can," because the worries that you have and the things that you were stressed about back then are just so unconventional. I wish somebody had said, "Hey. Adulthood. It's awful. There's stresses about rent, stresses about needing to make a doctor's appointment, and also, you never know when your next job is gonna come in."

And I wish that I would've known that...I mean I guess I did. From thirteen, I was doing stand-up, so I guess I was always a kid in an adult world. I always felt more mature than the kids that I was around in school, so I think that's just because I think I'm better than everyone, but I don't know.

School was never something where I feel like it was shaping who I was. I feel like I was who I was in among people who either got it or they didn't. I never had a huge group of friends that was always around. I just kind of floated between groups of friends, and there was never a concrete group of friends that I had until I grew older and then started doing stand-up and moved down here, and then I had friends.

Bonnie: Yes, then it's like, "Oh, these are my people."

Joey: Yeah, the people that understand, who want to do the
          same thing I want to do.

Luke Benward

Luke: I went to public school every year. From kindergarten
          until I graduated high school.

Bonnie: But you were also shooting a major film almost every
          year on average.

Luke: I tried to kind of have one project a year growing up. I also
          loved football, and I played football every season from
          third grade, I think, until after sophomore year when I
          stopped.

          It was pretty normal. I started kindergarten, and I also
          started acting. When I started school, I would tell my
          teachers, "Hey, I'm an actor. If I leave during the year, I'm
          going to keep my grades up. I just need you to send me
          the work. I'm going to get it done, and then I'll be back
          in class." I'm kind of obnoxious, and I'm an artistically
          brained person, so I'm going to whistle and hum and sing,
          and you're going to have to call my parents and tell them
          Luke's disrupting the class. And I'm going to get good
          grades. That was kind of what it was, pretty much, the
          whole time I was in school.

          I'd come in and out. When I changed schools, that was
          another thing that was kind of hard, because I had gone
          to school with kids who were used to me leaving and
          coming back, and it wasn't weird. I had to leave in my

junior year. I had friends there, and there were a lot of kind people there, but they weren't used to it, and they saw it as kind of like, something to make me different from them, you know. Especially at that age, if someone's different from you, they're against you. Then you get out of high school, and you realize, "That's not really how it works. People are people."

Bonnie: Life is not high school. Yay.

Luke: Right. That was the worst. School as a whole was cool, but I'm happy to be out, for sure.

Bonnie: And you had studio teachers when you were on set who helped you keep up with the legal requirements of being an underage kid still in school and keeping up with your schoolwork.

            People need to understand that young actors still have to keep up with their studies, but they're supported in that by having set teachers.

Luke: Yeah. And I'll say, I notice now, I can work a thirteen- or fourteen-hour day, and I'm fine. I'm good to go, I'm drinking coffee, I'm chilling, I'm doing my work, and I'm chilling in between takes. When I think back to how tired I was when I was a kid, it's unreal. Because it's the school part that really makes it so hard.

            Three of those hours on set have to be school. In between takes you're getting rushed and everyone's screaming, "We're not going to make our time; get him in school. The sun's running out." It was way too much. That's another reason I'm just so happy to be done with that. Because that made sets just catch fire.

Bonnie: I remember we met when you were seventeen, and your family had just moved to Burbank, and you and Dove were cast in *Cloud 9* together.

And then we all got to know each other, with our families on set for that project, and I remember seeing you up in the snow in the A-frame doing your homework in between scenes.

Luke: It was the worst. Especially, too, on that set. When we were on the slopes, getting from the schoolroom to set was just as treacherous as trying to snowboard the half pipe. Yeah, I had some rough...I'm not going to name any names, but I had some rough set teachers too; that really didn't make it easier on me.

Bonnie: I've noticed that there can be a really wide range of quality of set teachers. Some of them are just outstanding. And some of them you just wish were doing something else.

Luke: Yeah. To make any real project, film or television, it takes a team. You all have to be team players and get your job done but also respect the person next to you and that they have a job to do that they're trying to do just as hard as you are. It goes for actors, it goes for producers, and it goes for set teachers. Yes, you have a job, keep it in the guidelines, but it's a team effort, so also just try to help each other out.

Dove Cameron

Dove: Right, well...let me give you the breakdown of my school-
          ing experience. First of all, my dad told me that Johnny
          Depp...I think (a) didn't go to college and then (b) never
          finished high school, or something like that?

          Ever since my dad told me that, I was like, "Whatever."
          I don't mean to discount school. It's just that my brain
          never ever gelled well with school, and you can back me
          up on this; you're my mom.

Bonnie: Yes, you started having issues with school in first grade.

Dove: I was a very headstrong, individual thinker, and I really
          didn't like that teachers thought they could tell me what
          to do. I kind of would in rebellion just sit in the back of
          the class and not listen to anything because I really didn't
          like that they were teaching me...I think my dad had a lot
          to do with this. He would always tell me, "Schools are all
          teaching the same thing all the way across America, and
          it's not individually tailored. So, sweetheart, you have no
          reason to twist yourself into the ideals of whatever." I
          just never really fit in with school. I learned more through
          experiences with people and travel and talking and lis-
          tening. I was such a listener. I loved words, and I loved to
          write and I loved a lot of things that are not things that
          you can only learn in school.

          I always like to preface what I'm about to say by telling peo-
          ple that. I really am an autodidact. I really am very curious. I
          love to read and look into things and learn facts, and I also
          have a good memory. Once you tell me something, I will

never ever forget it, and I'll never forget the intonation of which you told me it in. I never really had a problem with my strange schooling pattern, but basically I went to kindergarten; I went to half of first grade. My teacher and I didn't get along, so I dropped out halfway through first grade.

Bonnie: You were homeschooled.

Dove: Yeah, okay; you don't like dropped out. My mom doesn't like dropped out. "I dropped out of first grade; I was a problem child." I dropped out of first grade. I was homeschooled for the second part of first grade, and the first half of second. I thought, "I don't have any friends," so I went to the second half of second grade in public school. Then I did third grade in public school, fourth grade in public school, fifth grade in public school, and sixth grade in public school. Although I really only went to like half the days of school because we were traveling so much, and honestly, my dad would just say, "Do you want to stay home and eat toast?" I'd be like, "Yeah." He would always say, "Oh, those grades don't matter anyway."

Bonnie: Your dad and I had different opinions about school a lot of the time.

Dove: Then I went to half of seventh grade, and I was being really severely bullied, so again, dropped out, and was homeschooled for the second half of seventh. Then I took a placement test?

Bonnie: Yes, you took the Iowa test, which is not placement; it's about achievement—it's about measuring what you actually have learned.

Dove: Right, so I finished seventh grade, and then the test results showed, "Oh well, you've basically learned everything you need to learn for eighth grade too, so you can skip eighth grade." I technically did ninth grade online?

Bonnie: You technically did ninth grade online.

Dove: But like not really. Barely, you guys. Then I took a placement test, and basically it said, "You should be in college, but you can't skip more than one grade." Then they placed me in tenth, and I did tenth and eleventh in public high school in Burbank. Then I graduated a year early.

If you have an odd schooling pattern because you are a young actor, don't worry about it. You can go to college anytime, and lots of us actors have weird schooling pasts. I promise you, guys.

Bonnie: Related to that, do you ever wish that you'd had a more normal childhood or schooling situation?

Dove: Yeah, I do. Here's the thing. What I really feel like I missed out on was a community. I really feel like I missed out on a social circle. Knowing people from kindergarten to seniors in high school, then having that hard time leaving for college, going to the same place every day, missing the school walls, and knowing the teachers by their first name. I really missed that experience.

I also miss—I really wish I'd gone to college. I wish I'd gone and lived in a dorm, even though everybody says, "No, you don't"—no, I want the bad experience. I want the bad experience of living in a dorm, having to deal with my dorm mate, and hating them.

I wanted the normalcy, but it didn't fit in with the other life that I wanted more.

Also, the time that I did spend in school, there wasn't anybody else like me in school, and nobody liked me. Every friend I tried to make didn't understand me, and they all kind of excluded me because I was very artistic and odd. I was always a very odd kid. I would go so far as to say-I think a lot of people might think, "Wow, you have an ego," but no—I think this is very truthful. I was always a very intelligent kid. I really was pretty advanced for every age that I was, and a lot of teachers, and a lot of other kids didn't like that.

I'm saying this because I've met so many special, intelligent, advanced, incredible, impressive children through being in the industry and meeting these people who come to the live tapings and my fan signings. I see them, and they're so special, different, and charismatic, and they say, "I don't have any friends," and I say, "Oh my gosh! Of course, you don't. That's no reason to be sad, that just means that you're going to find your community later in life, and you have the brains to know that that's going to happen for you, and you don't have to worry or lament." There are so many kids out there that are special and different. They get bullied, they get left out, and they don't have friends, and they become the most incredible adults.

I always want to say that. You hear that all the time. People in the industry who were really bullied and had no friends in school, because they're different, and if you're listening to this, you're different. I just want you to know that's okay. You're going to be okay. Everything is fine.

People can hate you all they want, and you get to live your dreams. So that's that.

Bonnie: Yes, and just be patient. Have faith.

Dove: Yeah, exactly. I'm so passionate about speaking about this to those kids because I came home so many times from school and talked to you. I was like, "Mom, boys don't like me. I've never had a boyfriend. Girls all hate me. No one will look twice at me. Not even the freaks like me." There's always that weird section of kids where you think, "Maybe I'm going to be one of the weird kids." And the weird kids say, "You're way too weird for us." You know, I always want to speak to those young minds that are so concerned with that because Lord knows I was concerned with that.

I was lonely. I was a lonely kid. Now I have a great adult life.

Bonnie: That's beautiful. I know that that's true, and I love the message that you deliver with it. Speaking of school and going back to acting, how did you balance the school and the acting thing? How did that work for you?

Dove: It didn't work well. A lot of teachers take it personally when you miss school to act because I think a lot of people want to be in this industry. You know, a lot of teachers don't like when kids get involved in this industry.

A lot of people obviously want to be in this industry. Either for the right reasons or the wrong reasons or whatever the reasons, but a lot of teachers see it as sort of an insult. Sort of a good-bye to education and a hello to a fantasyland. I ran into that a lot. A lot of teachers said some pretty incredible things for an adult to say to a young mind that don't need to be mentioned here. A lot of teachers sort of tried to stop me from pursuing this.

In a nutshell, I can think of literally four or five different teachers who told me this. Basically, I'm throwing my life away, and education is the only answer, and how dare I insist on living a life otherwise. I wouldn't be surprised if your kid—or if you are the one who's pursuing a life in acting—I wouldn't be surprised if you ran into that as well. Not to turn this into a soapbox, but they're so wrong. They're so wrong.

That's obviously not easy to hear, and obviously these people have incredibly sad minds to try to be putting a child down. I wouldn't enter into the school versus industry conversation with open arms. I would definitely enter into it cautiously. Because teachers have the power to fail you. I was getting failed. Even if I was staying on top of my studies, I would miss enough school, and the teachers would get angry, and they would literally just fail me. You definitely have an opportunity to run into that.

I was going to high school in Burbank when that was happening. Although I have heard of some teachers being really supportive and letting you do your homework on the side, or homeschooling is always a fantastic option, or there are certain actor high schools. I was going to public high school, but there are certain actor high schools that are sort of designed so that you could be doing that. A lot of my friends went there, like Olivia Holt, Zendaya, and a lot of other Disney kids went to that one high school— I always forget the name of it.

Booboo Stewart

Booboo: School. I guess I started working when I was about ten. I would have been in fifth grade at that time, and that was my last year of school. My school wasn't very...I don't want to say they weren't supportive of me working, but it just got harder and harder. I can understand it. I'm missing loads of school. Each teacher was so different. You could have a great teacher who says, "Yeah, here's all your homework. Go. Learn."

It's such a learning experience. You get to travel and stuff. I guess toward fifth grade it got a little harder because your school gets harder, and you're learning things that you need to learn for the rest of your life. Luckily, I was finishing that, and I was just going to be homeschooled. So I started homeschooling, and from middle school on, I homeschooled all the way to the finish. I finished school when we were shooting the *Breaking Dawn* films.

I actually finished school right when I came back because I was just trying to get it all done. I was like, "Come on, dude. You're homeschooled; you can just knock it out. You'll have so much free time up here." We were filming in Squamish, Canada. It's kind of, I don't want to say in the middle of nowhere, but it's beautiful. All the amazing hiking...but at that age I just wanted to play video games, I guess. I just told myself to finish my school.

Bonnie: How old were you when you finally graduated?

Booboo: Seventeen. Yeah. Seventeen. Done.

Bonnie: Something that a lot of kids want to know from people that they really admire was how was your school experience? Was school hard for you?

Booboo: Yeah.

Bonnie: The whole social thing. Bullying and all that. That sounds like something you may have just sort of sidestepped. Do you feel like you did or maybe not?

Booboo: In a weird way, yeah, because I kind of skipped over that whole part of my life. In elementary school and fourth and fifth grade, in school I just kept to myself really. I would always go play make-believe with my friends. It kind of makes sense.

Bonnie: Because you're an actor.

Booboo: It really, honestly, made sense. The Lord of the Rings came out, and I would be Aragorn, and my friend would be Legolas, and we would run around the field finding orcs, literally. I love sports, but I never was on any teams. I did martial arts. I just kept to myself and played make-believe and drew on everything. I was always drawing.

Bonnie: That's what a lot of creatives do in school. They don't necessarily fit perfectly in, and so they kind of run off into their imagination somehow.

Booboo: Yeah. That was great to me. Fantastic.

Jessica Marie Garcia

Jessica: Middle school was tough for me because I was always overweight, and I have psoriasis from the knees down. I'm just a furry girl. I mean: moustache, unibrow, side-burns, I have it all. If you can have hair there, I have it. That was really hard. You know what I mean? In middle school, your parents aren't going to let you shave your legs and I was like a woolly mammoth.

I feel like I got my comic chops from middle school, and I have a tooth gap, oh my God. People would say that they'd kick field goals all the time. That was really tough for me. Those were the hardest days for me, just because I didn't want to go. I went to a private school, so we all wore uniforms and just being able to see girls who fit it better, and I had no choice to wear these things.

It was sad, and that's when you start realizing that you're different. That's when I really started doing comedy, and doing plays was fun because it made me a part of something that I wasn't. I did chorus too. Being busy like that really helped. High school, I was a little bit the same, knowing that I could start over, but I think my junior year I completely changed.

There was a switch that changed in me where I just did not give a crap about what anybody thought, and I felt myself changing knowing that…I think my mom said it to me. She was like, you know that high school is four years, and then you never see these people again. No one wants to be the person that peaks in high school.

When I would go to high school, and I wasn't the ones picked in the plays, I was always in tech. I did music for *Les Mis*. We did the most beautiful *Les Mis*. I did wardrobe, so I can make things. I can do a lot of things. I was a well-rounded actor, but I never got picked. I remember being on stage to audition for something, and I didn't say a word.

I think we had to do something from *Medea*, and I just stood there in front of an entire room of seniors. I just stood there. I thought, "I guess I can't act either, so I guess they're right." Then again, you have that voice inside of you that says, "No. Why would you ever put someone else's opinion of your dreams on your dreams?"

This person doesn't care if you sink or swim. Why put that on them? Now, it just feels so great that the people that said that about me are literally contacting me, trying to hang out with me or get a meeting with someone I know or their kids watch me. That's hilarious to me. There's nothing better. There's no better revenge than success.

Just knowing that...Again, you have to believe in yourself. You're worth it. That's my biggest message when I was losing the weight, when I was struggling with this. I am worth it. If somebody says, "No, Jessica. You can't win an Oscar." I would think, "I can, and I will because I'm worth one." I think that's what's so hard, is people get scared to believe in themselves that much, and it shouldn't be that way. You should be your number-one fan. You get to be whoever you want to be.

Bonnie: I love that because it's your life. Nobody else gets to tell you. It's like the fabulous children's book *Harold and the*

Purple Crayon. Just pick that crayon up, and draw what you want to step into.

Jessica: If you go back and you listen to interviews with Steve Jobs or anybody that you care about, you read about their struggles, and they were never these kids that weren't made fun of or these normal people.

Bonnie: Nobody that I know has reached a high level of achievement without some struggle. You don't see that struggle. Let's be honest. People don't put the struggle on Instagram generally. We see the exciting bits, but we don't see the private moments of doubt and fear and pain and the struggles that went on, when they were in middle school and high school, to get there. Even when you landed here, and you were eighteen, it didn't all fall into place for you.

Jessica: No. I was waiting tables the first two seasons of *Liv and Maddie.* You don't know what's going to happen to you. The struggle is real and alive. I was taking pictures with kids while I was handing them their burgers. That just is a reality of life.

Bonnie: That's amazing.

Jessica: Again, this is what I love to do. This was what I was meant to do.

Sarah Jeffery

Sarah: Initially, I did commercials when I was younger, so that was manageable. Then as time went on, and I got *Rogue,*

I realized how much work it would be and how hard it would be to juggle school and work and then dance as well. Often kids have extracurriculars that they don't want to let go of. I was lucky enough to go to an art school where most teachers were quite understanding about maybe getting the homework ahead of time and doing it at my own pace.

It was huge. I somehow managed to maintain good grades, but it got to a point in grade eleven...Grade eleven was my last year in actual school where I felt, "This is getting a little bit too hard for me to be in five hundred places at once."

I don't know if people realize how much it can be even for kids. It's so much. My mom and dad and I decided online school would be the best option for me. I was doing it independently without a tutor, so it does take a lot of work ethic; it does take a lot of concentration. I won't sit here and say it's easy. It's really difficult. I like school, but school has always been a struggle for me. It felt like it was the best option for me at that point in my life.

Bonnie: Online school is a great option for a lot of kids—in some cases, even if you're not trying to manage a professional career while you're still a kid. Sometimes the social thing is enough of a challenge that you just want to step away from that. Online school makes that a lot simpler.

Sarah: It really does. In my experience, personally, artistic peo-ple can struggle with anxiety, and that's not something I'm afraid to talk about. I think that's a huge thing.

It's very common. I see that more and more as I get older and dive into this industry deeper. It's a huge thing. Having all of that on your plate, on top of anxiety that already existed, it was sort of nice for me to just do the online thing, even though—I will not lie—it took a lot of work, a lot of dedication, but ended up being worth it for me. That might be a good fit for some people.

Brenna D'Amico

Brenna: I like homeschooling because you can go at your own pace, and there's not as much pressure. I've always loved homeschooling. Always, always, always. It was really cool that there was no conflict or issues throughout filming and school, with being an actor and being homeschooled. I'm really grateful that nothing conflicted like that.

Bonnie: A lot of actors homeschool, and some go back and forth, but it's neat that you were always doing it. There wasn't a huge transition and change, which can be challenging for some kids. You're not even going to need to take the CHSPE; you'll just graduate, because you're on top of your stuff.

Brenna: Ah, I'm so excited; thank you. I'm really excited, because I do go a bit faster, just because I want to graduate so bad, so I'll be able to work more.

Bonnie: That's the cool thing about homeschooling, because you can do it at your own pace. To be able to really legitimately graduate high school at sixteen is huge. Congratulations.

Brenna: Thank you so much; thank you.

6

Challenges

IF YOU LOOK at the Instagram accounts of successful young actors, it can seem like their lives are an endless stream of fun and excitement. But they would be the first to tell you that social media presents a very edited highlight reel. Every human on the planet has challenges, and fame and success don't change that.

Auditions, rejections, the transition to adulthood, the uncertainties of the industry, financial uncertainty, the stress of fame, staying camera ready, learning how to manage yourself on a set, looking different, disappointment, anxiety—these are just some of the challenges these young actors, as well as their peers, face on a regular basis.

Some of the wisdom that has come out of learning how to deal with these challenges:

- Have patience and perseverance
- You are good enough
- Question everything
- You've got to really love it
- Let go of what you can't control
- Your body is your instrument

- Feel the temperature of a set before you get too casual with people
- The more you audition, the easier it gets
- What's meant to happen will happen
- A support system is very important, even if it's just one person

Read on to see what these young artists have struggled with, and sometimes still struggle with, and what they have learned to do that helps.

Victoria Moroles

Victoria:　Auditioning has been one of the biggest challenges for me. When I'm at work, I'm so much more comfortable. I face challenges at work, but you have people who are there to help you for that. It's all a collaborative thing. When you are auditioning, you kind of feel alone, and that's a really hard thing to face. I could totally see somebody, especially first starting out, having that feeling, because I had that feeling.

Like I said, realize that everybody else is there for you. It is still a collaborative thing like it is at work; it just may not feel like it as much, because the preproduction part of it is very separated, and casting directors and producers may feel very far away, but it's still very collaborative. If I think about it in that perspective, I don't feel so alone.

That's been a really hard thing, and it helps me if I just think about it like, "You are going to do your part. They are going to do their part. If it matches up, great. If it doesn't, then it wasn't meant to be, and somebody else can step into this a little bit better. Whatever fits a little bit better." Another really big challenge that I've had is to remind myself to have patience, because I can't stress enough how much you need that.

Bonnie: Patience is probably one of the most critical assets for an actor.

Victoria: Yeah, because it's inconsistent, and it's a lot of waiting. Even when you get on set, you are waiting. Can I just tell you? You are never going to stop waiting! Waiting is part of the deal, so just figure out what to do with that time. If you go crazy over the couple of auditions you had for the week and you are just sitting there thinking about it, which we all do, you've just got to remember to have patience. I started out here when I was twelve, and I didn't get anything till I was fifteen.

Bonnie: That's really normal.

Victoria: Patience and perseverance, just staying determined. There are times definitely where you feel like, "Do I want to do this?" It's like anybody else's job or craft. It's a love-hate relationship, but in a good way.

Bonnie: You love what you do. Clearly, this is the right work for you. But even for anybody who is on the right path doing the right work, there are going to be days you feel like, "What am I doing?"

Victoria: I know a lot of artists who have those days, and they take them very seriously and dramatically, because, I don't know what it is about artists, but if you just feel not motivated one day, you feel like you are not on the right path, and you are not on the right journey. But it's okay.

Bonnie: It's because you guys are just so dramatic!

Victoria: I know. Exactly. My mom says, "Honey, it's fine. You are just having a bad day. It's okay." You are going to have bad auditions. You are going to have really good auditions. You are going to have good days at work, bad days at work. It's all going to be there.

Luke Benward

Luke: There's a lot of rejection. You would think I'd be used to it, but I feel like as a kid I didn't really realize it. I didn't realize that they were saying no. It was out of sight, out of mind, I guess, with me.

            Yeah. It's not like they email you back and say, "This is why he didn't get the role...blah, blah, blah." You just don't ever hear. But when you have the rent and the car payment, you start to take the nos to heart a little more. That was kind of a new thing for me.

Bonnie: That's part of the transition. Being a young adult working actor.

Luke: Yeah, it was definitely a weird transition, and I kind of went through a phase of partying, for sure. And I kind of got stuck in that. You get stuck in this routine. And because you're stuck in that same rut, you start to think that you don't really have it. It's a hard struggle.

            That was definitely a big transition for me as a kid: becoming a young adult. It kind of just brought it back to the base level, I feel like, when I got a note one day that I didn't look healthy.

Bonnie: That's a wake-up call.

Luke: Yeah. I thought, "Pause. Let's get this back on track." It was rough.

It was really an introspective experience. I took my time and figured out: What am I doing, and why am I doing this? Because I wasn't happy. I was auditioning and not liking it and just trying to get through the auditions. I had lunch with Mitchell Gossett one day, and he really gave me some great advice, and my parents were obviously there and talked me through it, and really what it came down to was I just wasn't creating. I had kind of lost sight of that.

I was trying to prove myself, and I was trying to impress people, and be the leading man, and be the guy that gets the room's attention, and that's what I was focused on. I was focused on winning them over, and I was focused on putting on a good performance.

I finally got down to the fact that I am good enough; this is the only me I have, and I have been good enough, and I will continue to be good enough, as long as I work and work and just be honest and experience life.

Bonnie: Yes. And honor yourself by taking care of yourself, which is part of the learning curve for any young adult, I think.

Luke: Totally. And that's kind of what I had to go through, and I definitely came out the other side stronger, but it was a roller coaster.

It was me just a lot of times alone with myself, and those are some of the most enlightening kinds of experiences, when you can just really dig into why you're upset, why you're sad, why you're mad, why you're alone.

I mean, from an acting perspective, that gave me time to get down to the nitty-gritty of me.

Bonnie: And getting in touch with that bedrock truth for yourself would have to make you a better actor as well, and would have to make you a better artist.

Luke: Totally, yeah. It only makes it better. I found that when I had peace in that area, I was really able to let loose and experiment. It was a cool transition.

Bonnie: A lot of the best life lessons are like that. It's awful to be in them. But it's great to have had them.

Luke: Exactly. You've kind of got to go through the fire a little bit, and it wasn't anything extreme, but it was definitely some fire for a little bit.

Joey Bragg

Joey: Teachers, especially in California, don't make that much, and my parents had to support a family of four, and we couldn't pay the mortgage if just my mom was working up there, and my dad was paying rent down here...

Even with what you're making on a show, it's still hard. It's still a hard business to make a comfortable living out of. And I have always felt much more mature than I've looked, and so I felt when I was seventeen, it was okay to have my parents move away. In hindsight, absolutely not. I wouldn't have had them do that, but when you're a seventeen-year-old kid, and your dad says, "So we don't have very many options here. One of the options is I move away, and you live by yourself," of course, I'm gonna be like, "Animal House! Sure. Let's do it."

I miss my family, and I don't see them all that often…I have a very strong connection with my parents, and I call them every day, but you just never know what's gonna happen. And there are so many people trying to take advantage of you, and everybody seems like they have your best interests at heart, but none of them do.

Bonnie: Well, they have their own best interests at heart, which may occasionally align with yours, but you cannot bet on that.

Joey: Yeah. I think that a lot of kids don't understand how it works. They don't understand how the world works, don't understand to look out for their best interests, don't understand to question everything.

Don't ever take anybody's word for what they're saying. Think about what they're gonna get from you, and just think about the decisions you make because everything can affect you. If you are caught doing anything bad— for example, if you're caught smoking pot somewhere, and you're on Disney Channel, that could end your Disney Channel show—and then that will look bad.

I know I sound so cynical, but I was such a special circumstance. I don't think I would be here if I didn't start in stand-up, and I didn't have that amazing first Disney Channel job, and I don't know what I would be doing, but I don't think it would be staying here and hoping that something happens...I already have so many good connections that I feel like I at least have people around me that believe in me, and I can do something. And I'm full of myself enough to feel like I can do something and people want to listen to me. But I think there's no betting. You never know.

Bonnie: Right, it's not like you're not signing up for college.

Joey: Yeah and then getting a bachelor's degree in economics, then getting a job. There's no certainty. And a lot of kids move down here when they're very young and work and work and work, and then there's nothing else they can do. Because that is all they know. They didn't really go to school. As much as you want to say, you were six, and you went to studio school. And then you get to the real world, and there's nothing else, and your only option is waiting for that one perfect job to fall in your lap.

            It's just such a weight to put on a child's shoulders. There are so many kids that have to then support their families, or their families can't pay rent, and I know so many kids that were responsible for paying rent, and that isn't a thing somebody like that should have to experience at such a young age.

Bonnie: That's a whole other conversation. In the state of California, that's technically illegal. The child's money is the child's money. It's not family money, by law, but in most of the rest of the country, whatever the kid makes, it's fair game. It can be family money, so some families feel, "We're gonna be rich." But actually that's against the law here in California. It doesn't mean that people don't break that law, of course.

It's a moral dilemma that people face who come out here and give this their shot. Almost every room I'm ever in, if I just say, "So where is everybody from?" Almost everybody is from somewhere else. Most of the people in the industry are from somewhere else. They're not from LA.

Most of the time they're just good, normal people who are trying to do right by their kids.

Joey: Yeah. And I think that there are a lot of kids or a lot of actors that will get that Nickelodeon show or will get that national commercial and then think, "This is it." And there's, first of all, nothing that proves that you're going to ever work after that again.

There are some great documentaries. *You're the Guy from That Thing* is an amazing documentary about character actors and how they got started. You'll know all of their faces, but probably not their names. None of them, for the most part, are safe. None of them can pay rent for X amount of years in the future. Living paycheck to paycheck when you never know what job's going to be giving you your next paycheck is something that only a certain amount of people can handle.

Garrett Clayton

Garrett: There've been full years where I haven't filmed anything...some things have clumped where they've come
out at the same time, but I filmed them years ago. I just
had a movie called *Don't Hang Up* come out, and I filmed
that two and a half years ago.

I finished filming *Don't Hang Up*, flew back on a plane
at 1:00 a.m. from London, got into LA the next morning, took a nap, and went to rehearsals for *Teen Beach
Movie 2*. And mind you, when I was a waiter, working from
5:00 p.m. to 5:00 a.m. every day, I was studying my lines
while I was washing dishes or folding napkins and rolling
silverware. I had a few regulars who became friends of
mine. They would run lines with me when I'd get a break.
I would be eating in the back alleyway on my ten-minute
break, studying lines. I think a lot of that, as well as, not
every job pays incredibly well, and you have to make that
money last until you get the next one.

Bonnie: People underestimate that. They think that everybody
who does movies and TV just makes buckets and buckets of money, but that's really often not the case. Then,
whatever you do make, a lot of it goes right back out to
your team and to taxes.

Garrett: Especially now. These days, the market is so vast that the
money in it is so watered down.

So nine times out of ten, the things you're doing aren't
going to be paying you a lot of money. It's the money
that you're going to have to figure out how to make last
a couple months.

I know myself and 99 percent of my friends: we're all hus-
tling, all the time, constantly. When I'm doing a job, I'm
still sending in self-tapes and working on other auditions
while I'm working on projects that are very time consum-
ing. I can be on set for fourteen hours a day, on camera
all day, and the one hour I get a lunch break, I'm working on an audition so I can go home, take another two
hours to film the audition, let alone if they need a song
or something, and then maybe I'll get to sleep for four
hours. Maybe.

Bonnie: Every young actor I know, when they're filming on location, and they're away from their home setup, they've
got some clever way to set up an iPhone, and there's
duct tape involved sometimes, to get those self-tapes,
because you don't stop doing that.

Garrett: Yep. You don't stop anything. That's the thing. So, with the
market being so vast, the money being watered down,
you can be working your butt off and still feel, sometimes, like you're not getting as much of a reward, but if
you really love the work...and that's the thing, when people tell me they want to be an actor, I say, "You've got to
really love it. You've got to really love what you're doing
because a lot of the time, it's going to feel like you're
working your butt off to get just centimeters ahead of
where you were." It seems like there's a lot of reward in a
lot of it, but there's not, because nobody's there with you
for the other hundreds or thousands of auditions you've
done.

There's struggle with every aspect of what we're doing,
whether it's being on set and people's egos or being
on set and they're fighting about a line of dialogue you

have to say, and then everybody thinks you're aggressive when really other people are fighting about things. There could be issues that people don't even think come up...I know some actresses...there've been arguments on set between producers because they want their eye shadow to be a certain color.

The thing is that can be an issue. People in any other job would say, "Are you kidding me? People fight about that thing?" Whether it's a camera angle, a line, or somebody's attitude on set that day—maybe somebody's having a bad day, and they're taking it out on everybody, and then that halts production for another two hours. Somebody's late to work, and then that pushes everything, and then they have to reorganize the camera shots. Then you're there four hours later, still waiting to do the same thing...

It can be anything. That's why I always say you've got to really love it, and you've got to be really patient.

Cameron Boyce

Cameron: I've had plenty of challenges. For a couple years on *Jessie*, I did not know how to handle fans at all. And I didn't like when they stared at me. I didn't like when they whispered about me. I didn't like when they came up to me. It all made me very uncomfortable. And for a while, I felt, "I don't think I want this. I don't know that I can handle this."

And it came down to the simplest stuff. My parents would say, "Hey, I'm going to the grocery store; you want to come pick some stuff out?" I'd say, "Eh, no, I'm okay. I don't feel like getting recognized. I don't feel like dealing with that right now." So for a long time, maybe two years, I was very much, "I don't know how I'm going to handle this." A year before, I was playing basketball after school with my friends. That was my life. And now, everywhere I go people are looking at me, and I'm this thing, you know what I mean?

Bonnie: You become objectified at a certain level. When you become famous, people treat you like you're not a real person.

Cameron: They literally treat you like an animal in a zoo.

Bonnie: You're not really real.

Cameron: That's a great way to put it because...I feel like when I was a kid, I don't know if I let it happen or because I was a kid they just didn't respect me as much as they do now. Now I get, "Hey, my kid really likes your show. Thank you for doing that" or "Oh my gosh, I used to watch you as a kid," all these things. And they're really nice. I love it now. But back then, I think older people just felt like I owed them something. It was this weird, "You're a kid; I'm an adult. Take a picture with my kid." That's how it was. They never really said, "Hey, sorry to bother you," you know? It was just sort of like, "Hey, you're that kid, right?" That's sort of what it was. That was the worst. That sends chills down my spine.

           Like if you go to a zoo and you're sitting there and you see the cage and zebras or whatever, you point and you talk about it, and you take pictures. That's what I felt like.

Bonnie: You talk about the zebra in front of the zebra.

Cameron: Yeah. You talk about the zebra in front of the zebra, you
            point at the zebra, you point at the stripes, and you take
            a picture of the zebra, all without the zebra really know-
            ing or without the zebra's consent...

            That's what I felt like. I would sit at a table with my family
            at dinner, and I would see a family two tables down, and
            they would be talking about me; they would be looking
            over at me constantly, pointing, and I felt like an object. I
            really did. And that sucked. That was the worst. I've come
            to terms with that now. And I still get that a little bit. And
            when I do get stuff like that, I just remind them that I'm
            a human. When people are staring at me or sneaking...
            that's the funniest thing to me. When they sneak a photo,
            it's like they think I don't know they're taking a picture.

            Like really? I see you. But it is what it is. The other day I
            was sitting outside eating at some restaurant, and some
            dude so obviously, without my permission, came up as I'm
            eating and took a picture of me. And I put my fork down
            and I just posed. I literally put my arms out and smiled.
            And he was so embarrassed. He didn't know how rude
            that was or he should've asked me first. He didn't even
            think about it. And right when I posed and he was caught
            red-handed, he turned red, and you could see it click in
            his mind, "Oh, that's probably not cool." I don't like to say,
            "Hey, man, that's not cool."

            It is what it is. There are so many pictures of me on the
            Internet that are ugly. You can't control that. You've got
            to let that go. So whatever. And right when he saw me do
            that, he sort of was embarrassed and also grateful that I
            posed for him. It was the weirdest thing. I have fun with
            it now because that's all you can do. When it's a part of

your life and there's no way to escape it, you can hide from it as long as you want, but that's just going to make it worse. Just live your life, and people are going to be weird and rude and awkward.

I've gotten mothers who have asked me to kiss their daughters on the cheek. And think about that. If you asked anybody in any other scenario to do that...that's completely out of bounds. That's completely a no-no. That's not what you do. But they feel like they know me.

Bonnie: When you're on TV in somebody's living room, it's like you're in their house night after night for years.

Cameron: Oh yeah. I get told so many times. People say, "I feel like I know you because you've just been around."

Bonnie: It messes with people's sense of boundaries, I think, because they feel like they know you, so it should be okay. But the truth is they don't. You're not Luke.

Cameron: No, I'm not Luke. I'm not eleven anymore. I don't live in New York or on the Isle of the Lost. I live in Sherman Oaks. But they have no concept of that sometimes. And that's okay. It's actually really nice when little kids come up to me and say, "Wait, where's Dude the dog?"

Dylan Playfair

Dylan: Challenges in the journey so far...I sound so privileged just saying that.

When I first came into Vancouver, I was an athlete. I was really big. I weighed about 210 pounds. I'm 180 now. I lost a lot of weight, and it was after I finished playing hockey, and I was in this headspace of, "I'm not going to train for a while, so I don't need to be physically fit at all." My agent, when I walked in, the first thing she said was, "I don't need another pretty-boy hockey player." The second thing she said was, "I need you to get in better shape." I thought, "Oh my God. Really?"

She was not beating around any bush. She said, "I've got these three roles that you'd be great for, but I can't submit you because you're too out of shape." That was a challenge. I was getting in shape and staying in shape. Your body is an instrument. You have to be really cognizant of how your health is because that's your tool.

Bonnie: It's not just female actors who have to pay attention to this. Male actors have to pay attention to it too.

Dylan: Absolutely. You've got to perform. If you're not feeling good, that can affect your job. That was a challenge for me because I kind of associated those coming from hockey. I just thought that those were concerns that athletes had, and now that I'm an actor I don't need to think about that stuff. I was really quickly reminded that, no, that part of the game has stayed very much the same, my friend. If you want to book these roles, you're going to have to look this part. That was a challenge that I remember being frustrated with myself over. I had given up for three months and gained forty pounds. I was able to get over that pretty quickly.

What's been hard? I've been really lucky; so far, it's been nice. Losing that weight was...it was a lot of time spent on bikes.

Dove Cameron

Dove: Some of my challenges have been not getting caught up in some industry cattiness because I am a very open person, and I'm obviously a very talkative person. I have boundless energy—some would say it's too much—and I don't really believe in hierarchies or being higher or better or worse or lower than other people; I never really have. A lot of people have a huge problem with that. It started when I was in school, when my teachers thought that they were more important than a seven-year-old because they had the power. It's always people who want to have power.

I don't mean any disrespect. Everybody has their own brain, their own experiences, their own life that they want to lead, and the way that they want to do it. I'm not saying that my way of doing it is better or worse; that's just my way of doing it. I have definitely stepped onto some sets or met some people who do not agree with my way of doing it. I believe that everybody is equal— if you're an extra on set or you're the lead and you've worked on twenty films this year or you get paid eight times more than an actor who's working more than you or whatever—I don't think that anybody is better than anybody.

That has kept me really happy because I don't want to be better than anybody. Oh my God, I don't want to be better than anybody. If I came home at the end of the day and my sense of satisfaction was because I was better, higher, more important, more rich, or whatever than that person, how sad would I be? That's not where my value comes from, and so I've run into some problems with that. I've run into some problems when some people maybe think that I'm out of my place or something to believe we're all equal. That's definitely been a challenge for me, and I've learned that lesson. I definitely was a little excited when I first started in the industry, and it's a sad truth...you do kind of have to enter every set with caution and be a little bit quiet until you find your place... or not. It depends.

If you want your experience to be that you're utterly comfortable from the first second you step on set and if somebody has a problem with that, whatever. Live your life. If you're not doing any harm and you're just having a good time, live your life. But if you want there to be no problems, I would say enter every set with caution and feel the temperature before you...just sort of let loose and be yourself all over everybody.

Bonnie: Brilliant, hard-earned advice.

Dove: I just believe that bugs are equal to clouds are equal to animals are equal to the president. That's just how I feel. I don't know why you would want to feel otherwise, but... that was my biggest lesson I think.

Booboo Stewart

Booboo: Just looking so different from everybody else has always been a challenge. When I was younger, it wasn't an issue. Modeling was great; looking different is fantastic. Dancing, it's fantastic. In the acting world, it's so difficult to look different but to fit in. It's such a weird thing, and I've definitely found my niche here and there doing different things. Certain parts have pushed me in different ethnicities and that's been fantastic. I think one of the biggest hurdles is just reading things and just thinking, "Why am I doing this?"

I literally will ask my dad, "Did they look at a picture of me?" Honest! I just asked him that last week. I just auditioned for this thing last week, and it's an awesome script. I'm glad I went in. I liked those casting people. I've always done great auditions with them. Fantastic people. I love them. But I asked my dad, after I read the script, "This is great, and I love it, but do they know what I look like?" Literally, "Do they know what I look like because I don't think I could do this role at all." But hey, you never know.

I think that's been the biggest hurdle, just getting over that factor.

Bonnie: Over something you have absolutely no control over. We all look the way we look, you know? We're a certain height and color mix and everything else.

Booboo: Exactly. That's been just frustrating. It's still frustrating. Just last week I was frustrated. I have to memorize seven pages of dialogue and, really, I don't want to give a bad audition, so I'm going to give it everything I have for something that I kind of know is not going to happen.

Bonnie: I think about that a lot because when I was still going out with Dove and she was auditioning for stuff a lot before she got booked up for a while, it felt like, "Why are we spending hours and hours memorizing these lines when you just don't fit the description at all?" But you have to.

Booboo: You've got to do it. At the end of the day, it's practice. Practice at auditioning because that's another thing. And practice at just being an actor. Memorizing lines. The more you do it, the easier it gets. That's how I get over that I guess.

Bonnie: I think that's a really good point, and it's just so true. The more you audition, the better you get at it.

Booboo: Literally, that's it. And self-taping is the worst. I hate self-taping. It drives me nuts. I self-taped, again, last week and met with the director; then he gave me notes, and I self-taped again, and when he was giving me notes and we met for breakfast, I said, "You know what? I'm going to be honest with you. I've only booked one thing off of self-tape. It was the thing I did in the Arctic. I'm doing a self-tape for this, and I just want you to know that I'm doing the best I can. I literally have my dad holding his phone and trying to flip the sides all while trying to be an actor with me, and I'm looking at a speaker. I'm literally looking at a speaker. Just so you know, that's what's happening."

And then I would edit it and put the scenes together on Movie Maker off of a Samsung phone.

My dad's doing three things at once. I'm acting. I'm trying to give you the most honest work. My friend, Ben, says, "Anyone good at the profession is good at making it look easy."

Every actor can act. I can act out a scene, but it's one thing to be an actor, and it's one thing to be an honest actor. Right now I'm being an actor. For that audition. I was like, "I'm acting this."

Bonnie: Because it's not perfect conditions. Not at all. I do recommend a tripod.

Booboo: Oh, that is a great idea. I don't know why we haven't thought of that. All these years. A freaking tripod.

Bonnie: It frees up your dad's hands to turn the pages of the sides.

Booboo: So he can turn pages. He's throwing them on the ground. I can hear them. Like…"crrrrr." You can hear it in the audition. His voice is three times louder than mine because he's holding the camera right next to his head.

Bonnie: That's the other thing. You can step away from it when you've got a tripod. This is my hot tip for you.

Booboo: Good idea.

Bonnie: I'm helping Dove do a self-tape later today, so we feel your pain.

Booboo: Oh yeah. So annoying. The only upside to them is that you can get not a perfect audition but something you really feel comfortable about. You get more than one shot at it, and I think that's good, but it's also hard.

I don't know how you feel about doing it with Dove, but self-taping with your family is hard. It's really hard. I would much rather…I like going in. I like meeting the people, and I like auditioning with a stranger. It's easier.

Bonnie: It is hard. But she and I have developed a way for it to be as easy as it can be for her. Basically, I just try to be as invisible as I can be and to downplay my personal energy because she's so familiar with me. But it's not ideal.

Booboo: No.

Sarah Jeffery

Sarah: There are the obvious challenges, like really, really wanting a part and then it not going your way, or the hardest part is when you get so close, and it's between you and someone else, and it doesn't go your way.

It can take ages, and it's nerve wracking. I'm always sitting on the edge of my seat and waiting for that phone call. Sometimes it's not the phone call you want. I have this mind-set that what's meant to happen will happen. If it wasn't that part, maybe it's because a part down the road is yours and you wouldn't have been able to do both.

Definitely. Everything has its mapped out path. Keep that in mind when it seems really difficult. I know it's hard. It's not easy to feel that close and then not be the one, but it will work out the way it's meant to work out. Additionally, I personally have suffered from anxiety. I won't lie about that. That's not something that I'm ashamed of at all. This industry can be anxiety provoking sometimes.

Bonnie: Life all by itself is anxiety provoking enough, and then you add this industry to it, and it's like fuel on the fire.

Sarah: Totally. That's when support systems come in, no matter if it's one person who you can rely on; it's very important to be able to have someone to go to and to take a break from all of this when it all gets to be too much. Those have been my struggles. It's definitely not easy, and I have times where I think, "How am I going to do this?" but it's absolutely worth it, and you come out a stronger person.

7

Rejection and Haters

REJECTION IS A fact of life for any actor, even successful ones. And haters—unfortunately—are a fact of life for many kids in school as well as for many people online. The more visible you get, the more your light attracts all types of people—including some who seem to take joy in trying to dim that light.

Young actors have to get very good at dealing with rejection and haters, because they have to deal with that energy so much. So many become masters at it.

Here are some words of wisdom from these young artists on dealing with rejection and people who want to bring you down:

- It's never about you when they put you down.
- If you understand where they're coming from, you can find that maybe their life isn't as good as yours or maybe you have something that they really want, so they're mad at you.
- As long as you are happy with what you are doing, who cares if anybody likes it?
- You realize that you can't please everybody.
- I just kind of observe and move on.
- They are behind a screen...they wouldn't say it to your face.

- Step away for a second; step away from the phone. Go out, take a walk, and look at the world that we have: trees; connect with the earth, and then come back to your piece of technology.

Brenna D'Amico

Brenna: When people say hurtful things on my Instagram and when I see that, I don't let them affect me. My mom has taught me to never let that affect you, and it never has because she's taught me so well.

When I see those things on my Instagram, I delete them. Not because they affect me, but because I do not want that type of negativity on my page. Then the people that support me get really upset and start arguing and fight back and forth. I don't want that anywhere near my page. I don't want them to be upset, and I don't want to see that.

I really try to stay positive and just realize that it's not about you. It's never about you when they put you down. I really can't stress that enough to people that do get bullied. I just think it's awful that it happens, but you need to understand that if you are comfortable with yourself and you love yourself, and you know your family and your friends love you for who you are, then it shouldn't affect you.

Bonnie: I'm still just appalled at how free some people feel to just say the nastiest things online. It's like you're not a real person, you know? To be really, really clear, it's just not about you. It is about the person making the commenting. It's an absolute reflection of their internal condition.

Brenna: Right. It really does appall me seeing some of the things
            people say to amazing, amazing kids that do not deserve
            it. I've been so lucky to not have to deal with that on a
            daily basis. I feel so much and so awful for the people
            that do but don't deserve it. Nobody deserves it.

            Don't fight it. Don't fight them, because one, that's what
            they want, and also...it's not healthy for you. Don't let
            that negativity in your life. Just push it aside, and fill the
            negative space with positivity and positive thoughts.

Bonnie: How do you handle rejection? Rejection in terms of rejec-
            tion in the industry. For example, when you go in and
            you have a role that you really want. You want it, and you
            worked so hard to prepare for it, and you don't get it.

Brenna: When I eventually hear the no, I didn't get something, or
            don't hear for a while, I kind of figure it out that I didn't.
            For every one, I do my best. If there's one thing that
            I didn't like about it, or one thing that I would've done
            differently, I think about it for five minutes, and then it
            leaves me. Then I completely let it go, and I think for me,
            that really helps with just doing your best, going in there
            hoping you killed it and you rocked it, and then just let-
            ting it go and not thinking about it again.

            I've always been that way, and I love that I'm like that as a
            person because it helps me so much. It helps me so much
            with rejection because when you think too much about
            something, I feel as if it's not healthy for you—when
            you overthink, like oh, why did they say no, why didn't I
            get this?

Think about it for maybe five, ten minutes, and then let it go. Just don't be too hard on yourself. I've never been too hard on myself, so I think that's what really helps me deal with rejection.

Bonnie: A lot of people—artists and actors especially—we can really get in our heads and we can circle around in there a lot. What are your go-to methods for getting out of your head?

Brenna: I get in my head a lot. Luckily, I've never let that ruin something for me. I'm obviously still practicing not letting it, but what I think is if you think over and over again, "I'm not going to mess up these lines because I know them"; I just reassure myself that I know what I'm doing and I know these lines, and I know what type of character this is.

I think it's all about confidence. Confidence is the key. Not confidence as to where you think you're better than somebody else but confidence where you know you're comfortable with yourself. I think that's really the key of learning and not getting in the way of yourself.

Booboo Stewart

Booboo: I think you just have to not care because you have to know that they took the time out of their day to think about what they wanted to tell you, and they've logged on, they went to your page, they've seen all the great things, and they just want to throw in their hate mail. It's such a dumb thing. I just don't like it. I try to avoid it. For every handful of good things, there will be two handfuls of haters, just because people want to hate.

Bonnie: That's something I really struggle to understand. Do you
have any advice for young fans who are struggling with
bullying or haters?

Booboo: Yeah. Maybe some advice would be just try to understand
where their hate is coming from, maybe. Why would
someone want to hate on you? Like what's the reason?
And for everybody that answer would be different.

You know what I mean? I think if you understand where
they're coming from, you can find that maybe their life
isn't as good as yours or maybe you have something that
they really want, so they're mad at you. That kind of gives
another outlook. I kind of feel bad for them. Let them
keep doing their thing. Don't let it frustrate you.

It's about them trying to express their hate, or their dislike, or want for something you might have. Just try and
understand where they're coming from first.

Joey Bragg

Joey: I get a lot of haters because I speak my mind a lot. I never
want to have to feel like I'm being anyone other than
myself. I don't know. Especially with a Disney Channel
show, you get a tweet that says, "You suck." Then you're
like, "Wow, that hurts", but then look at their page, and
it's an eleven-year-old girl or you see somebody that
doesn't like your show and you click on their page, and it's
just some dude sitting behind his computer that watches
Disney Channel for some reason.

I'm learning that as long as you are happy with what you
are doing, who cares if anybody likes it? I don't care. I do a

podcast, and I never think anybody is listening. You do it for the people that like it or you do it for yourself.

Bonnie: You don't want to live an inauthentic life for the sake of trying to have everybody like you, because the truth is it's never going to happen. Not everybody's going to like you.

I want to loop back really quick because I'll bet you there's a bunch of eleven-year-old girls who are listening to this who are feeling very insulted right now. The fact that somebody might be an eleven-year-old girl doesn't discount the validity of their opinion.

Joey: No, but if a little kid ran up to you on the street and said, "You suck," you wouldn't be thinking about it for the next couple days. You would be like, "That's a kid that is running up and just voicing their opinion."

Bonnie: Yes. They're probably just having a bad day, and who knows what's going on in the background?

Let's talk about rejection. This bears discussing because rejection is the lifeblood of this industry. Hollywood is Rejection City.

Joey: Exactly. The hardest part about going up and asking a girl out is the possibility of her saying no, but then you go and you're acting and you go and you work on this audition and you do the character for them, and then you don't get a no, you just don't get anything. You don't get a call, you don't get an email; you just don't ever hear from them again.

I like that aspect of it, because especially now, my biggest advice to people that are auditioning and trying to be actors is as soon as you're done with that audition, look at those sides, rip them up, cuss out the character, do whatever you have to do to just have the most negative outlook on what you just did. Then just block it out of your mind, and be surprised when that email for the callback comes.

Dylan Playfair

Dylan: I have the funniest set of fans because I did *Letterkenny*, which for those of you who have seen it, will know it's very much rated R...so unless you're eighteen or your parents say it's okay, be aware. Then there's *Descendants* and *Some Assembly*, which is targeted six to twelve.

So I've got this weird dichotomy of fans. The only real haters I've ever had are the fans of *Letterkenny* who see *Some Assembly* or who see the kids show and are like, "Wait, what? Why are you on a roller coaster in a tank top dressed as a clown? I don't get it." I think that for me, I have pride in that because it's range. To me, if I can do this job well and I can do that job well, it obviously means I'm doing something right. To be honest, a lot of haters sit behind the protection of an anonymous screen.

Doesn't take a lot of courage. In fact, I think it's pretty gutless. I keep that voice in the back of my head. I just try not to pay attention. In anything you do, you're going to have people who resent you because either they couldn't do it or somewhere along the line they found satisfaction bringing other people down. That's one of those personal decisions where you go, "Do I really care? Do I really care about what someone I've never met and probably never will..."

You spend time to do that. You spend time to write that review. That's your life, man. That's what you're going to do with it? I feel like I've heard those words from someone somewhere along the way. But, do something with your time.

It's funny because you'll see so many positive things on the Internet and that one negative jab will sit with you. If every nice thing that somebody said to you meant as much as the negative things, people would walk around on sunshine. For the most part, people have been great, especially on Twitter and Facebook and social media, which is now how you interact with fans. In the last ten years, it's been the new thing. I try to, if there is ever hate, every five or ten, "You're great, this is awesome, love the show," one out of ten, I'll still take it. It's a good batting average.

Jessica Marie Garcia

Jessica: Oh, social media. Things people have said about me, and the things people have problems with about me physically are just hysterical to me. The gap in my teeth offends so many people.

It's so offensive. It's funny because I can always tell the age range of my haters because if they're under fourteen, they hate my eyebrows. My eyebrows are too big for them, but if they're over fourteen, they're "on fleek." It's very one or the other.

They're not saying, "I'm unsure about your eyebrows." They're freakishly large or they're incredible. That's how that is. How do I deal with it? I find it funny now because really I'm so much older than the majority of them that I look at their profiles, and they're like seven years old, and their bio is, "Live, laugh, love God." They quote a song about not judging other people. Then they're writing, "Go kill yourself."

Just saying horrible, horrible things, but it's really just for a reaction. I feel blessed to be this age dealing with it rather than being Dove's age or being younger, like Tenzing's age and having people say this because at my eighteen years old, my nineteen years old, I would have probably been at a different place with it. Right now, I mean, you're not going to tell me I'm not good. I care more about if you told me I was a bad actor—which you won't because I'm not—but if you think I'm ugly, I don't care. Whether or not someone finds me attractive, I don't put my worth on that.

You realize that you can't please everybody. If you are like the most gorgeous, best actor in the entire...there's nothing anybody can say about you, which I feel like that's your daughter. You see that, and you hear comments, and you just think, "You're obviously wrong." I just can't take it seriously. I can't. I get more mad when I see comments where they're saying hurtful things to each other.

When they're saying it to me, they're looking for attention. Someone doesn't love them enough wherever they are. That's the sad thing. It has really nothing to do with me.

Bonnie: People really reveal themselves by how hateful they can be. It's like—wow, you're just broadcasting your internal condition more than anything else, much more than actually making a comment on me.

Jessica: That's because they don't think we're real people. We're unattainable. I was going to the beach with a couple of my girlfriends and someone had tweeted something about Shelby's outfit on the beach with us. It was like, "Wait, what? Who is that, and where are you?"

           You can become unsafe. I had someone at a movie theater approach me way too closely, and he was yelling at me about what shows I was on, because kids had asked for a picture. I had never felt so vulnerable before in my life, and that's when that hater thing becomes a different thing, and it becomes an unsafe thing.

Bonnie: I noticed this really early on with Dove. There's something that happens to people when you become a public figure. All of a sudden, you're not a real person anymore. It's like you literally get turned into an object. You become objectified. That's a really scary thing. This happens not just with fame but also with racism, with sexism, and with other things like that...

           You can treat objects like they're not people, because they're not people in your mind. You can say and do the most horrible things, and that's where it gets weird.

Jessica: It's unfair. You sign up for working and you sign up for doing the job and becoming a character, and I understand that that comes with taking pictures and signing autographs, which is something that I love to do personally. I think it's so much fun. But when it becomes a safety issue...that doesn't mean that you get to invade somebody's personal space. I remember Anne Hathaway said that she was at a party, and someone just came up to her and said, "I hate you."

She said, "Oh, hi. Nice to meet you." You shouldn't feel like you could be able to do that.

My whole life, I've had this thing where strangers talk to me all the time, just all the time in general about anything. I typically welcome it because it's funny. I've met some very interesting people. Now, it's just really scary, especially with all the scary things that are going on in the world now. You have to be so wary of it.

Bonnie: It's funny because a lot of kids who want to be actors, what they're really enticed by isn't necessarily the work so much, but it's the idea of it. The idea of the fame. The trappings. The truth is it's a very double-edged thing. You get to do what you love to do, make a living doing your passion, and there's nothing more beautiful or wonderful than that, but there's a shadow side to it.

Jessica: You hit the nail on the head with that. I think the majority of people that come out here are looking for fame. I could care less if anybody knew my name as long as I was working.

Bonnie: And respected by your peers maybe? That's the important thing to most actors.

Jessica: Absolutely. When you asked about idols, I think who I should list is Allison Janney and Frances McDormand. Those women I think are just the most incredible actors, character actors, actors in general, and they are the ones that, unless you know them for their work and appreciate them for their work, you probably wouldn't know them by name. They are widely respected. And they have so many awards between them. That to me is more enticing. I don't care if I'm in a magazine. I'd rather be revered. You know what I mean?

A lot of people do come for fame and all that; a very small percentage of people get it.

Luke Benward

Luke: It's such a weird thing to me. I have trouble understanding it, really. So I kind of had a hard time empathizing with them, I guess. Everyone's going to have an opinion of anything. This is a horrible example, but say a man kills a hundred people; odds are there's someone in the world who will say, "Maybe he didn't do it," you know? And you say, "Yeah, but there's video," and they're like, "Who knows? Maybe he didn't do it."

I feel like there's always at least a person that's going to disagree and that's going to have an opinion that's different from yours, and it's fine. It's fine for you to express your opinion; it's fine for them to express theirs back to you, of you, if they want to. I don't know if I really deal with it as much as I just kind of observe and move on. That's what they choose to do with their life, and it doesn't really affect me at all. You can't control that. You can't control how they feel or how they express how they feel. It doesn't change anything you're doing.

Sarah Jeffery

Sarah:　When I first started noticing it on my page, I thought, "What? People are saying these things. That's not true!" My heart would hurt a little. As time went on, I would realize, "They actually don't know you. They don't know anything about you really. They only know what's on the surface."

Second of all, they are behind a screen. They wouldn't say it to your face. I think it's important to look at yourself and remember who you are and what your values are and try as best as you can to tune it out. Don't read the mean comments if you can help it.

Bonnie:　Not Googling yourself daily is a smart thing. Don't do that.

Sarah:　Don't do that. You will find things you don't like. I get it from various projects I've worked on. Sometimes it's because my character has a romantic relationship with a guy who has many fans, and it's borderline threats. It's very scary. It's so strange. It's just a crazy thing. Also, for me, there's a balance on social media with sharing your work life and your home life.

Bonnie:　Yes. There's got to be a line. Everybody that I know who manages social media successfully creates some sort of boundary where some things just stay private.

Sarah:　Totally. Before I started acting, that was not really a concern, because that's what I used Instagram and Twitter for. But we have a very unique job, and so we have to be sort of careful. That will save you from additional peering eyes that you don't really want.

Bonnie: I think that's good advice for anybody really. It's easy to overshare. Once anything is out there, it's out there for good. Think twice about what you share, and keep the things that are really important to you private.

Sarah: I think it's nice to have a private life and a public life.

Victoria Moroles

Victoria: I personally have a very hard time with social media. In this industry it is a very crucial thing to have. My sister is in emerging media and communications media. All of it, she loves it. I think that it's great. I think there are very useful purposes for it. Then there are the downsides to it where people do put out really negative things. I try to create my own energy, but I do feed off of other people's energies a lot. I try to do the minimal amount that I can get by with for my job, and then kind of keep it at that, because it's draining.

It is the future. I've literally gotten auditions that have a breakdown asking how many followers do you have? It's to that point. A lot of us are realizing we can't run away from this. It's not that I don't like it; I really do, but there are a lot of negative things about it. People out there who feel some part of their life is not full and fulfilled, and they may be insecure about certain things, what have you. But they feel like they need to project the negativity onto other people. The thing is now we can do that with no consequences.

It's so hard for me because if you were sitting with somebody face to face, you are not going to say that to them. You might, but probably not. Just the fact that people have the ability, society has the ability to project that stuff onto other people...it may be on your phone through a piece of technology, it still gets to you.

Bonnie: It's like somebody who's anonymous has a megaphone to speak to anybody that they choose to in the world. It's not a very healthy environment.

Victoria: It's not. I hate it. I do love Instagram because it's really creative, and I'm pretty good with it. I try to post every week or so. It's only because it's creative. I like photography. There are a lot of different things you can do with it. That's probably my main one. I don't really do Twitter that much. My sister handles my Facebook, and it's hard because so many of my friends and everybody else in this town say, "You have to do it. Come on. Let's do it."

I'm like, "I just don't like it." It's never really a good answer, but it's an honest answer. I try to get by with what I can, because I understand that this is important for my job.

Bonnie: Actors don't really get to escape anymore, but it sounds like your strategy for dealing with what can be a negative online environment is just to minimize your contact with it.

Victoria: Yes. That's what I was going to get at. If you are feeling overwhelmed by it, which everybody does, you don't have to do it.

Step away for a second; step away from the phone. Go out, take a walk, and look at the world that we have: trees; connect with the earth, and then come back to your piece of technology.

8

Audition Advice

NEED SOME AUDITION advice? These young actors have a *ton*! And they are generous in sharing. The following pages contain some serious gems, but to get you started, here are a few highlights:

- Always bring your headshot and résumé, even if your agent already sent it to the casting office.
- Don't take yourself too seriously.
- Bring your sides into the room, even if they are completely memorized.
- Casting is on your side. They want you to do well.
- If you can't book the role, book the room.
- Go to show your work, not book the job.
- Anything beyond your work has nothing to do with you.
- Don't put too much pressure on a single audition.
- Be off book (come in with your lines memorized).
- Remember that it's not personal.
- Be patient and persistent.
- Have fun with your auditions.
- Don't overprepare.
- Listen and react honestly...be present.
- Be on time.

- Don't apologize.
- Be nice.

Dove Cameron

Dove: First of all, always bring your headshot and résumé because I have been sassed so hard, and I'm not going to say by who, but basically, "If you don't have your headshot and résumé, go home, and come back when you have one. I don't care if your appointment is at four." Some people just won't take you. Always have your headshot and résumé. And I would say, "Print your headshot in color." People respond better to it.

You know, don't take yourself too seriously. It's a good balance between doing everything perfectly, and if you forget your lines and mess up, you can totally go back and do it again. It's not that you should be a robot in the room, but when you walk in, say hi to the casting director. Be personable, but don't be too personable, and I've made this mistake too, when I'm like, "Where are you from? What are your hobbies? Mine too. I like your highlights." They're just—"Okay, sit down, do what you're supposed to do, and then get out." You know, just be personable. Ask them how their day is. You'll definitely stick out more than the people who don't do that. People respond to nice people, and casting directors are people too.

I would say, "Bring your sides with you because no matter how much you think you're off book, you're likely to forget." I still forget my lines in auditions, and they will be much more forgiving if you just look down rather than having to get up and leave the room to get your stuff.

Obviously turn your phone off, all that stuff, and try to be different. I remember booking *Barely Lethal*, and I went in, and I had had a lot of coffee that day, but I remember meeting my director Kyle Newman for the first time, and I was obsessed with him because he's like a fourteen-year-old in an adult's body. I remember he told me, "Just mess around. Impress me. Do something different." I was like—okay. So I sat up on the chair, and I got up, and the whole audition—my girl was very frantic, or that's how I thought she was at least—so the whole time I was sitting up on the back of the chair, then sitting back down, then crossing my legs, then I would get up, and I would lean on the chair, then I would run around, and then I'd sit on the floor.

He said, "You realize I can't tape you if you're doing that," and I was like, "Yeah, but I could tell that you liked it, so I kept doing it." You've got to do something that the girl who just left and that the girl who is coming after you is not going to do, or the guy. You know I'm speaking as me. Do something different, and that doesn't mean come in wearing an eye patch. Don't do that. Just make weird choices. Make something that the casting director hasn't seen because that's what they're looking for. If they're looking for something that they've seen a million times already, they would have chosen the person ten people ago. They're looking for something to blow their minds and to be different, so be different.

Dylan Playfair

Dylan: Funny, my very first audition…I blacked out in the room; I was so nervous. I blacked out. I saw the green *X*. I blacked out for a bit, and I remember coming back to, and they're like, "You ready?" I don't know how long it was. I kind of stumbled back, sat down, did the scene, and didn't book the job.

I guess where the advice goes is, "Don't be nervous. If you do, do it your first time because people's memories are short."

I ended up calming down a lot. What I found with auditions was they really want you to do well. They really want you to be as comfortable as you can. They're hoping you're the guy or the girl. They're really hoping you can solve their problem. That, for me, was such an aha moment. So much of going to auditions is stressful and intense and intimidating. When you have that little voice in the back of your head going, "They want you. They're praying you answer their question," it makes all the difference. That, for me, became such a confidence-boosting moment, when that realization made sense. "Of course, they want you to be the guy." They're trying to make a project. They need to fill these roles. If they don't do their jobs, they don't get to be in casting any longer. You and they are working together to solve a problem. I think if you have that mentality, it becomes so much less daunting. They support you. They want you to do well.

Bonnie: They want you to win. They're on your side. They're not out to get you.

Dylan: Exactly. It's hard to see that because sometimes you come in at the end of the day, and there's just one guy there, and he clicks "Record," and that's it. It can be really dehumanizing, and you think, "Don't you know what I did to get here?" They're in the same boat. You've got to recognize you're in that same environment with them. They're there too. They've gone through what you're going through. So recognize that, and take a, "We're in this together man" versus "Here I am again." It becomes so much less stressful that way.

I was in Toronto finishing up season two of *Letterkenny*, and I got a self-tape audition for *Descendants 2*...actually Harry Hook was the original self-tape I sent in...I sent it in, and on the same day they said, "Okay, not that one, but try this guy (Gil). Let's see how that tries on for size."

I didn't have any makeup or anything. I didn't have any real taping set up, but I had instant coffee and my iPhone. I took the instant coffee, and I made eyeliner. I blackened my eyes because on the sides it said they were Goth...

We didn't know what we were auditioning for. It was just "Goth pirate." So I had blackened my eyes and my buddy, I think, we duct-taped my phone to the hotel TV, and that was how we taped it.

It was so Canadian bootleg. If anyone had walked in, they would have been very concerned for what Andrew and I were up to. I turned my shirt into a tank top to try to look more like piratey, and I had coffee on my eyes and we were saying these weird lines. Anyway...we had fun with that; it goes back to that thing with the casting director. We were comfortable. We were having fun. We were not precious and nervous about it.

Bonnie: You felt safe.

Dylan: I felt safe. That was it. That was my audition process. It
            was shocking because after I sent the tape in, I found out
            about two weeks later that I booked the role.

            They booked me off the tape. I was shocked. When I talked
            to Kenny (Ortega) about it, I said, "I only auditioned twice
            off tape, and I didn't redo any scenes. I just did the two
            guys." He said, "We knew who you were." I had come in
            and read for *Descendants 1* for Chad Charming, which is
            played by Jedidiah Goodacre, so he knew who I was, and
            they made a bookmark. Since that time, I've done *Some
            Assembly Required*, which is a kid's show. They were able
            to call the casting for that and watch that footage and
            made the decision based on that. You never know what
            little project is going to come back to pay out for you.

Bonnie: That's so cool. That's a great illustration of the fact that
            serious casting directors track people.

Dylan: They do. People talk about not booking roles and how
            it can be so deflating. You've got to understand that if
            you're not booking that role, book the room at the bare
            minimum. Go in, and build a relationship because you
            might not be right for that role, but if you impact that
            person, you leave something with them that they think
            about. It happens all the time. Someone will see you on
            a project or see you in the room and go, "Not right for
            that, but you know what? There's this other thing." I think
            that's how you build a career. That's how you really grow
            and expand, when people start thinking about you in
            breakdowns.

Bonnie:　　And they're just looking for a place to put you because they really believe in you. I love that. Honestly, you could have said, "Oh, life's horrid. I didn't get Chad Charming. I wish I had been in that cool *Descendants* movie." But guess what? You're in the next one.

Dylan:　　Right? And doing a role that Jedidiah did…I loved that role, but I had so much fun doing Gil. At the time, it's exactly what I was. I was so bummed out. I wanted so badly to come into Disney, and when it didn't work…it sucks not getting jobs. Everyone knows that. To have it come back around, that's how it works. Sometimes it doesn't happen two years later. Sometimes it's five or ten years later. You got to know it's out there.

Bonnie:　　It could be three years later. Dove had a pilot that she came so close to booking the lead on when we had been here about a year and a half. It was this big drama. Seven rounds of callbacks. So stressful. The final round, she was in the top two, and she didn't get it. It was the most grueling, rough experience. Three years later, the director on that project was the producer on another project, and she booked a leading role on it. He never had forgotten her, and when she showed up for the next project, it made a difference. You've just got to believe that these people don't forget you.

Dylan:　　Two things. One, Dove is amazing. Two, I had forgotten entirely that Wendy Japhet, who produced *Descendants 2*, and I had an almost identical experience. I had auditioned and gone right up until the very end of a project called *Speak to New York*. They ended up going another way. When I got on set and met Wendy, first thing she comes up and gives me a hug and says, "You were so great on *Speak to New York*. I'm so glad that we finally get to work together."

Garrett Clayton

Garrett: I always go back to the one thing that keeps me sane. You can't go to book the job. You have to go to show your work. Because anything beyond your work has nothing to do with you.

Your height, your weight, what you look like, your ethnicity, your background, all of that, it is what it is. So you can bring a very fleshed out, well-rounded character, and you know everything about them, and you can live and breathe as them and tell this room full of people this character's whole story that you made, but at the end of the day…I can read something, and this guy next to me, metaphorically, is going to go in right after, and he'll read the same lines, and it'll come across completely different.

I've gotten many calls where they say, "We love him. It's just not the direction of the character that we're looking to go in." That's okay. So, anything beyond the work has nothing to do with you.

It feels so personal. I mean, I've heard friends say they've lost jobs on their hair color. They've literally called and said, "Oh, we're looking for a brunette." Then dye the hair!

So, I mean, there are those moments that happen, and you just have to say whatever. Most of the time, it is what it is. You just have to prepare as well as you can and know that when you leave that room, you did everything you could. That's what we all do. We walk in the room, and we give it everything we have. Sometimes it's just not what they're looking for.

If you do well in the room, they're going to know that you're good at your job regardless. Just because you're not right for that part doesn't mean you're not good. It just means you're not right for that part.

Bonnie:　　And you've had experience with people being impressed by your work, the work that you were showing, and not booking you for that original role, but for something else, either later or in the same project, right?

Garrett:　　Well, *Teen Beach Movie* is a prime example of that. I read for Ross Lynch's character, initially, and then they called me back and said, "We think he'd be really good in the role of Tanner. Can he come back and read Tanner, but do what he did as Brady?" I said, "Okay." So, I went back, and I did that, and then I ended up going through to the end and getting the part.

That's a prime example of you just have to show your work, and sometimes it'll work in your favor, and other times it won't.

If you do well and if you come in the room and you have an easy demeanor, they're going to read that. If you're going in and freaking out, they're going to see that. If you can't handle going into an audition space, how you going to handle crying in front of sixty people behind a camera while you're pretending to be alone in a room?

Thomas Doherty

Thomas: So when I started going to auditions, I'd be petrified, sweating, couldn't breathe properly. Butterflies. Do you say that here—butterflies in the stomach?

Nauseous, horrible. Then you've got to go in and pretend you're someone else. You just can't, because you're so caught up in your own feelings and emotions. So you've got to just go in and you've got to experience all of that, I think. There's no point in someone telling you not to, because you're going to feel it regardless.

You've got to go in; you've got to just bite the bullet. You're going to be nervous. You're going to be petrified. You're not going to know what to do. Your focus is going to be all over the place. Your mind's just going to be, "Am I saying this right? Oh no, I shouldn't have said it like that. You're still in the scene, what are they looking at? Why are they looking at the paper? Oh no, should I look at…Oh no, jeez, I just looked at the camera, oh no." It's going to be like that, I'm sorry. It's going to be like that for you guys. But it's just experience. The more you go in, the more competent you're going to be, and the more composed you're going to be.

For me, the thing that changed was it was actually a video of Bryan Cranston I watched. He says he was getting himself all worked up over auditions and then it came to a moment where he realized, "I can't do anything more than what I can do. So I'm going to go in…" Obviously learn your lines; know everything. Create this character yourself; do what you think the character should be. Be open to any constructive comments or any criticism that they might give you. Then once you do your audition to the best of your ability, when you leave the room, that's it. You left the room, and there's nothing else you can do.

Bonnie: Let it go.

Thomas: You can sit for hours and days and weeks, but it's just completely redundant. It's not doing anything apart from making you feel not nice inside. So yeah, the best advice I could give you is to meditate. When you meditate, you get in your body, you get out of your mind, and you're much more composed. You're much more present. When you're more present, that shows on camera. You can see when someone's not in the moment. You can see when someone's in their own mind; they're in their own thoughts. This isn't the only audition you're ever going to have. There are going to be thousands of auditions. There's thousands of possibilities out there. Don't put everything on this thing.

I've done it, you just work yourself up, and you put all this hype into this thing. Then when you put so much hype into this one audition, you don't get the best results. Almost know that it doesn't really matter in the grand scheme of things. If it happens, fantastic. Amazing, exciting. If it doesn't happen, that's okay, because there's going to be another one next week, and then another one after that. Then another one, another one, another one.

So try and get out of your mind; get into your body. Make peace with the feelings that you're going to feel when you start. When you start to feel anxious, when you start to feel nervous, make peace with it. It should be like, "This is going to happen."

Then eventually you'll start to think, "Do I need this? Do I need to feel like this? Do I want to feel like this?" Then gradually you'll start to be able to kind of get out of that mind-set.

Bonnie: It's almost like the more you audition, the more your body and your subconscious gets the message. Like, "Oh, I'm actually going to survive this." You keep not dying in the room.

Thomas: I think there's an amazing line in *Fantastic Beasts* with Eddie Redmayne. I watched it when I came over from Scotland a couple of days ago. He says something along the lines of, "What's the point in worrying, because if it's going to happen, it'll happen, so why make it twice as bad?" You know, when it happens, deal with it, but why worry...Baz Luhrmann says worrying is as useful as chewing bubblegum or something.

Brenna D'Amico

Brenna: Relax. Be comfortable; be confident when you go in there. I would say what really helps me is before I go in, I think of my character, and I write down what the relationship with their parents is and what their hobbies are, what their characteristics are, and what they like and what they don't like. What kind of foods they like, what kinds they don't like.

That really helps me dig deeper and to just be comfortable playing and portraying this person. Get to know them, and create something behind them, not just go in and say the lines.

Personally, I'm always off book, and I think that helps me stay connected more, and without looking down at my lines so much. I would just say go in there and relax. People need to kind of take a moment before they go in to go into that character. Don't just play the character; be that person. Become that person.

Bonnie: That's good advice. You know, Dove got chewed out once for walking into an audition without her sides, because she had completely memorized everything. They asked, "Where are your sides?!" She said, "I don't need them; I've memorized it." They were so mad at her, they said, "Well, what if we want you to do something on page three?"

Brenna: Right, always have them, and maybe always keep them at your side. I would say always go in off book, but yes, bring them in. Maybe have them at your side or put them on the floor next to you. Just in case.

Bonnie: Any audition tips for self-tapes? Because even when you're in LA, you still have to do self-tapes. Not everything is live.

Brenna: Right, and when I was taping, probably my advice for that is pretend the camera is not there whatsoever. Connect with who you're reading with, and it's all in the eyes. If you're being taped, they want to see everything in your eyes. I really, really think pushing that emotion out where they can see it is going to be your face, your eyes, everything. They're not going to be seeing your whole body, so I can't stress enough, portray those emotions onto your face and your eyes, and really connect with the reader.

Booboo Stewart

Booboo I think the way I look, too, is sort of different. Me just doing general auditions...it's such a, I don't want to say waste of time because the more people you know and if you impress someone, it's great, but I've done that. You know what I mean? I've done so many auditions to where it's like, oh well, you know, I'm not, sorry to all the white people, but I'm not going to fit into this family. Like the parents...this is just not going to work. Very rarely. What I audition for is sort of specific. Like it's a very specific person, I guess.

It's so frustrating, and it's a hard mental thing to get over. I don't know. It's such a hurdle. But it's not about you. It isn't. You could be amazing in an audition and kill it and feel great about yourself, but if you don't fit into the family, if you're not tall enough, if you don't have that best-friend quality enough, if you're too much of this, too much of that. I think once I started writing and once I started thinking as a director because I want to direct, it made me realize that it wasn't personal. You know what I mean?

It's not personal, and I always took it so personally. I was like, "Oh my God! Do they not like me?" Then you're stressed for your next audition because you're trying to be good. Putting too much pressure and awareness on something is not good. You just have to get over that hurdle. I still am. It's so frustrating. It's auditions.

Bonnie: Speaking of auditioning, do you have any audition advice for actors, or want to-be actors, out there?

Booboo: Yeah. I definitely do. I think the biggest thing is when you have an audition, I don't want to say don't give it everything you've got, but don't put...this is very hard to explain because I don't want to say don't try hard because obviously, yes, do all your work. Train as hard as you can. Be prepared as well as you can with the material given, but don't go in with all your energy full-on-blown stamina unless a scene calls for it because so many actors try and do way too much in the audition to show that they're a good actor instead of just playing the scene.

             You have to just play what you're given instead of trying to convince everybody that you are a good actor. If the scene's emotional, be the emotion that it calls for. Don't be overemotional because you're trying to be like, "I'm a good actor. I can cry. I can."

             Tears don't mean you're a good actor. You know what I mean? It's such an interesting thing because I've seen it with some friends. Yeah, they're good actors, but they have this opportunity, and so they're going to go in and do everything they can to get it, and it's like yes, but no, at the same time.

Bonnie: Because that's not really what the casting director is looking for.

Booboo: Yeah, just play the scene, and do what it calls for. That'sit.

Cameron Boyce

Cameron: First of all, I don't even know how many auditions I've gone on in my life. We always look at an IMDb page, and we think, "Whoa, this person has done six projects." Yeah, six projects is a lot of projects. But to get those six projects, you have to do like six hundred auditions. But people do four or five auditions and they're like, "Oh, I didn't get a callback. I feel so distraught, and I don't know what to do, and maybe this is not cut out for me."

No. Persistence is one of the most important things... I've been on so many auditions; it's crazy. And when you get that call that you booked something, it makes it that much better because you've put in the work, and you've put in the time, and that's sort of how it is. And every audition is a little different, so you can't really go in with a mind-set of this is how it's going to be, this is how I'm going to do things. You've got to sort of leave that at the door, and be flexible and roll with the punches.

But I think one of the most important things about auditioning...it's really rare that a casting director is looking specifically for a breakout star. What a casting director is looking for is the correct person to play this specific character; do you know what I mean? A lot of people go in with, "I'm going to be this big and jazz hands." That's not what it is. You have to go in and present your performance in a way that speaks volumes for that character and not specifically for, "I want to be the next 'this person.'" And a lot of people do that, and they go in thinking, "Well, if I play it like this actress..." it's not how it goes. Casting is almost always looking for somebody who just fits the character.

That's the most important thing, and that's always what they're looking for. And that's why you can't be super upset when you don't get things because there are so many times I've heard, "Oh no, we loved you, but you were too short." "Oh no, we loved you, but the freckles, it just doesn't really go with the south." If I'm playing a confederate kid, I look mixed; that's just not going to happen.

So it just is what it is, and you have to understand that. And when all the stars align, it's really special. It's very, very special. So you just have to be really patient and persistent. The other thing that I would say, and it doesn't contradict what I just said, but there are two sides to everything. Go in knowing that you're one of a thousand million people that they're looking at. So that's something that you'll have to think about and understand so that you don't beat yourself when you don't book things.

But leave them with a little something to remember you by. Just a little bit. Don't overdo things, because then they'll just remember you as the person who overdoes things, but just pick a line where, just do it a little different than other people would. And you might not be right for that character, you might not be right for that project, but they'll say, "Hey, you remember that one person? They might be good for this." And when you go in enough and you see the same people, you go to the same casting offices and stuff, then they get to know you.

Just throw in a little bit of personality somewhere. Just sprinkle it on. And especially if you really feel that you're just not right for the role, go in and just throw caution to the wind. Just do it. Have fun. That's the most important thing. If you're visibly nervous, and you're sort of like "I don't know if I'm going to do well," or you're questioning yourself, they're going to see that.

And honestly, if you go into an audition tomorrow morning, and that's how you felt and your script was shaking... that's going to happen. I was working on *Jessie* for I think five or six years, and I did *Gamer's* for another two, so I hadn't been on an audition in like seven years. I went in for my first audition in that long, and trust me, literally, the paper was visibly shaking. Single bead of sweat.

And when something is so important to you, you really want to do well, and you start putting pressure on yourself, you get crazy. But the key is just to remember that it's one audition out of a bazillion, and if you're supposed to book that role, if that role is really right for you, then you'll probably be in the mix. You'll probably be in there. So just don't beat yourself up because if you beat yourself up, you're going to get sick of it really, really quickly.

Sarah Jeffery

Sarah: Auditioning can be nerve wracking, I won't lie. It can be overwhelming. Sometimes when you get into the thick of it, you have multiple auditions a day.

You really have to jump from character to character and be able to switch your gears. For me, it's important to find your own process and what works for you, whether that's prepping tons before, whether that's not overprepping. For me, overprepping is something that I try to avoid.

Bonnie: Yes, that's a danger actually. You can get so in the groove of doing something that you can't veer out of that groove when you're given direction in the audition, and then you're in trouble.

Sarah: Exactly. You don't want it to become stagnant. For me there's a fine balance with auditioning, between knowing your lines and being comfortable with the character and overdoing it to the point where you can't break from your habits. That can be tricky to find, but as long as you're persistent and you keep trying that with each audition, then I think you're going to be good.

Luke Benward

Luke: This is horrible advice, but my advice is, "Try not to listen to advice." I feel like I would always hear advice from really great actors, and I'd be like, "Oh yeah, I've got to do that next time in the room." Then I'm thinking about the advice. You know what I mean? I get out of the room, and I'm like, "Oh cool, my audition was basically me making sure that I smiled the entire time." That's not what the audition was about.

I don't know. I feel like I've progressed as a person and as an artist to where I've started to realize that what I'm bringing to the table is so much different than what anyone else has or will bring. For me, to take a tip from someone who knows me personally, and someone who's like, this is what I see, this is what you need to do, is different. But for someone to be like, "This is what I think," and for me to just say, "I can apply that," doesn't really work for me in my situation…My agent, Mitchell Gossett, he studied acting.

He is a phenomenal actor as well. He's partnered with my mom to do some workshops in Nashville. He's giving me tips as well, but it's really about being true to yourself. If the casting director gives you something that you didn't expect, gives you something that was less than what you expected or more than what you expected, that's what they're giving you, play off it. I think people get hung up on choices they made beforehand when really what it comes down to is listen and react honestly.

Bonnie: Just be present. And listen.

Luke: Yeah. If I were to scream whatever I said next to you right now, you would be like, "Okay, maybe we shouldn't scream anymore on the podcast."

We would continue on, and if the casting director screams something in the audition or is saying something super boring, then that's what they're giving you; that's the moment they're creating.

Bonnie: I like it. See, that's good advice, Luke.

Luke: Thanks.

Victoria Moroles

Victoria: It's not very inspiring, but it really doesn't get easier. It doesn't. Not in a bad way, it's just like I was saying before; I started auditioning at thirteen, fourteen, brand new. Then I didn't end up working professionally for a couple of years.

I moved here when I was twelve, and I auditioned steadily for a couple of years before I booked something pretty... not pretty big but professionally felt like I was working. It's so crazy because auditioning is a whole other job in itself. What I think helps me when I'm auditioning is that I look at it like auditioning is a job for me too. It's another job. If I'm not working on set, then auditioning will be my job, one of the jobs.

If I have an audition, I look at it and I take it just as seriously as I do work, because first of all, it's actually a lot harder because I am way more comfortable on set than I am in an audition room.

When I was younger, I didn't think it was that important, but now definitely I'm always on time. People appreciate that, as you would if somebody was coming to audition for you. Also, once I looked at casting directors differently or had a new perspective on them, I started feeling different about auditioning, especially thanks to Suzanne Goddard-Smythe, who cast me for *Liv and Maddie*.

She's just a ball of sunshine. She was one of the casting directors who always believed in me. She pushed me hard...We would be getting ready for a producer session. She's like, "Okay, Andie, are you ready? Let's do it." She's pumping you up. Realize they want this too. They want this for you too. They want it for them. It's again a fifty-fifty thing. It makes me nervous when I go into huge producer sessions or director sessions. I'm like, "Oh gosh. All these important people are here." You've got to perform for them.

They really do want you to do your best. Genuinely. When you look at it more like, "Hey, I'm going to work on this piece of material the best I can. I'm going to bring you my version of it. I'm going to do my best. This is what it is. If it fits, great; if it doesn't, then it's just not meant to be. Once you start looking at it like that, it makes it so much easier, because you are not pouring yourself into it in a way that if I don't get this project, it's the end of the world.

If you do your best version of this character for them, if it fits for them, then great; if it doesn't, like I said...that's something really big that I've kind of tipped into, I think about it every time I go in to audition.

Jessica Marie Garcia

Jessica: Be on time. That's a huge thing. If you're in LA, leave at least an hour before, especially if you don't know where you're going. You're not going to find parking. Expect not to find parking. If you can Uber, great because honestly, there's so many things that happen on that day of your audition. Your tire. You get a hole in your tire. You outfit has got a problem, and it's the perfect one to go on the audition.

Your printer runs out of ink. Everything that's going to happen is going to happen, and you have to know that ahead of time. I have a lot of friends—God bless them—who are actors, and they have not understood this. They go into a room, and they are frantic. They are sweating. They can't think about the words because they're too focused on "Oh, I'm going to get a parking ticket." I've had this happen. You have to expect it. Be prepared.

Have your headshot printed and ready to go, and be prepared is my big thing. Know your words. If you have three pages, you should know them. Especially for me, if I don't know my audition backward and forward, I can't do anything with it.

If I'm thinking about the words, I'm not thinking about the character. That so easily happens as an actor. A sentence could be like, "I was going to school" and you don't even think about it. It doesn't even make sense to you. It's about really knowing the words, so as you go over it, you're like "Oh wait, I'm having a conversation."

Then not apologizing. That's a huge thing for me because again, I've been there when they say, "Oh, can you stand here?" "Oh, I'm sorry." "Can you slate high?" "Oh, I'm sorry." Don't apologize. Don't put the casting director above you. You are on the same level.

You're not going in to find a job—you're going in to act. If you're not realizing that this is a moment that you get to do what you love…if you're thinking it's a job that you're so desperate to get, that's going to read.

I'm telling you—every crazy audition story, I have had it. I've had people not even look up. I always say I get this thing, and I don't want to think it, because it's a minority thing…I have people that don't expect me to be good. They just don't. I've had casting directors before *Liv and*

Maddie. I feel like I've gotten a little bit more respect having that on my résumé. I hope so.

I'd go into a room and they'd say, "All right, when you're ready, start." Then all of a sudden I would start and there would be a shuffle and I'd call it the casting director shuffle where it's like, "Oh, she's actually an actor. I didn't know that." I go in there with confidence like I've worked on this. Whether or not I'm not right physically is not my problem.

I can't go in there thinking, "God, there's going to be someone better looking for this or someone who looks better. Now, I'm in this weird place where I'm not stick thin but I'm not this big girl. It's like I just have to be the best me. If they like it, great, and if they don't, it's not for me. I can't kill myself for that.

Bonnie: That is brilliant life advice—not just brilliant audition advice. I mean, that's all any of us can do, is just be our best selves, and it's either for us or it's not.

Jessica: One hundred percent. I think of it as just another minute to act. I went out for something yesterday that was so unlike me, and I was just excited that they wanted to see me for something that was so unlike me. I knew that there were probably people more innately born to play that role, but I was going to do the best I could do. I was fine with that. I went in prepared. I was off book.

I am telling you, if you are off book and care at all and that shows, that casting person is going to treat you 100 percent differently. They're going to know a real actor's in the room, someone came prepared, and they will react.

I don't care how indifferent you might think they are when you get there, it'll change their perspective 100 percent.

Bonnie: I believe wholeheartedly in that. That was our experience too, and Dove was always just committed to showing up with her sides memorized. If you don't, it's almost disrespectful. It's like, "I didn't care enough about this role and this opportunity to bother memorizing the sides that a bunch of other people managed to do, by the way." Right away, it's just a mark against you.

Jessica: Sometimes you have three in a day that have nothing to do with each other. You have a Nick Jr. audition and then an HBO crazy drama and then a commercial for orange juice. It's unreal, the difference. That's part of your job. Some people don't realize that the business part of this is so much of it.

That would be another huge advice point that I would give to actors who want to do this, is that as much as your passion is so much of it: it's a business. Are you saleable? Is this saleable? Is this current? How can I make money out of this? That's all anybody cares about. You have to know that—in a way, you are a product.

When I came here, I had to find out who I was 110 percent and be unapologetic about who that was. Know that this is Jessica, and nothing is going to change that, and you're going to like that, because they will try and change you. "No, you're this girl. No, you're this, or you would fit really great as this." No. People will respond to that, but you have to have that confidence.

Bonnie: Do you want to say anything about casting directors?

Jessica: Be nice to them. We talked earlier, that a lot of people put casting directors on a pedestal, that they put them a little higher above them, and that you should go into an audition being on an even level, but also know that this is their business and you need to be...to be on that level, you have to be prepared and be respectful and be ready with your material and take your job as seriously as they do because... there's not been a single casting director I've come across in ten years that didn't take their job seriously. I think that's so important and because of them, I have work.

Bonnie: They're so key to what makes something magic and successful. They really are unsung heroes.

Jessica: They really are. There needs to be an Academy Award for casting directors. You see these movies that you fall in love with, and someone had to decide to put them there.

Whether or not they decide to cast someone of color or make a female role and things like that. They're the reason that the turnaround is happening. I've seen more in this pilot season the words "Any ethnicity," which is wonderful because you then are deciding who the best person is for the role, and not necessarily do they fit that idea that you already had in place.

Bonnie: Thank you for saying that because the role-modeling thing is so huge, and I've seen you speak to this in other interviews that you've done—but to be able to see somebody in a role that looks like you...

Jessica: That's so true. I did not have that. Even when I tell you the women that I admire the most, not one of them look like me. I just didn't have that. In a weird way, it never deterred me though. I didn't ever think that I couldn't do it, but I know that a lot of people do, and I can see why. I remember being a kid, and I used to get my favorite movies because I was that generation who were online.

I would get scripts, and I would write myself parts in movies that already existed. That's what started my love for writing because I thought, If you're not going to write somebody who looks likes me, then I'll just do it. I think that again goes into "Be productive." As an actor, I think it's important to be as multifaceted as you can be and find other loves.

I can't wait to direct. I can't wait to have my own production company. I want to do everything. I think that's important as an actor, to at least respect what everybody does in a production.

Bonnie: The beautiful thing about this little piece of our conversation, Jessica, is that you may not have seen other people out there who look like you, doing the things you wanted to do, but because that didn't deter you, now you can be that for other people.

Jessica: That's insane. I get letters from girls that say things like that, and it just blows my mind. It's such a crazy place to be because you think it's a story that happens to somebody else. You don't think that's something that happens to you...that you would be that person for somebody. I appreciate it. I don't take it lightly at all.

9

Surprises

EVERY LIFE HAS surprises...things that don't match our expectations, or things that happen that we couldn't have ever imagined. The path to success in Hollywood is no different.

Sometimes these surprises are hard. Realizing that you may have to be away from people you love to pursue your dream can be a hard one, whether it's to shoot on location for a few weeks or months or to move to Los Angeles to be close to audition opportunities.

Sometimes the surprises are wonderful. Meeting amazing people and getting to work with your heroes can be a dream come true. Finding kindred spirits and community can be especially sweet for young artists who may have had a hard time finding that before.

Success and fame can bring surprises of every kind...it can be underwhelming and overwhelming. The impact your work can have on people can feel moving and rewarding, and the unwanted attention that can also bring can feel frightening sometimes.

Whatever we expect on our path, we can be sure that life will surprise us...

Brenna D'Amico

Brenna: I didn't expect to meet so many amazing people. Working with Kenny Ortega, that was so surprising. Kristin Chenoweth, meeting her. The people that I've met have had such a big impact on my life that it's just so surprising in the best way. And Dove. Thank you for raising such an amazing human being. She is absolutely amazing, and I love her.

The rest of the surprises have been when I did audition and not hearing anything for a while, like for three, four months. It was really crazy to hear, "Oh, you did amazing. We're gonna put you on hold." To hear nothing and then "You got the part. You're getting on a plane to Vancouver."

That was super surprising. It was exhilarating, but it was also super surprising.

Bonnie: It's funny because I think we always have an idea about what something's going to look like. No matter what it is…I mean, if you want to be a lawyer, you think you know what that's going to look like, which is why you want it. You think you're going to want it, because you think it is a certain way.

Many people want to be actors, and you have an idea of what that will look like, but generally things aren't actually what they look like. In the end, they're just what they are.

Brenna: Right. You have to leave home…for instance, my family, we are separated for a lot of the time, and it's super hard on us. My parents and my family are making so many sacrifices that I may not be able to ever repay. I'm so grateful for them.

It really is hard, but the sacrifices are so worth it. I'm just so grateful to have parents and a family that do support what I do, and that was super surprising for me when we realized, you know what, we're gonna have to go to California, and I have to leave all my friends. That was super surprising.

Bonnie: I would think so. That's another thing I have noticed when I consult with families whose kids are really talented, really passionate. Maybe they're not quite so far down the road. They're going for it. I say, "So you do know that there may come a point possibly, where if your kid is as successful as they hope to be, you may have to relocate."

Some people do manage to go back and forth. Literally, I can think of a handful of successful young actors who all live in LA now, but they're young adults at this point. For years they were able to just fly out once a year and shoot a movie or go back and forth a whole bunch. But even that takes a huge amount of flexibility on the part of somebody in the family.

If you're a kid, you can't go back and forth by yourself. You've got to have a parent with you. You've got to have a parent on set, and that can be really challenging for families. What your family's doing is what a lot of families do, which is one parent stays behind, and takes care of the house, holding down the fort, and the other one goes out with the young actor. Sometimes the siblings end up split up too, and that's not easy.

Brenna: It's not easy. Sometimes it gets super hard, where it's almost about to be too hard. Then I always think, this is a once-in-a-lifetime chance, and that kind of is what holds us down a little bit.

Bonnie: I think that's a good way to hold it. The comparison I've always used is if I had a kid who had Olympic-level talent, who really had a shot at being on the Olympic team for something. Would I not relocate so that they could train and have that chance? I would. These are special circumstances, and sometimes they do require some amount of sacrifice.

            I don't like to use the word "sacrifice" so much, because the truth is when you're a parent, you would do anything for your kids that you can. But not all parents, no matter what they want to do, have the resources to do what your parents are doing for you.

            They may truly want to, but not everybody can. I don't know any young actors here who don't understand what a great act of love it is.

Brenna: Unconditional love. I love them so much. I wouldn't be doing this without them. I really wouldn't. I'm forever grateful that they're doing this for me.

Booboo Stewart

Booboo: Being a part of *Twilight* at such a young age to a young adult, I guess. I ran into Cullen, one of the guys, at a comedy show yesterday, and we actually just talked about it for a split second before he had to cross the street. Being a part of that and being submerged in that bubble of crazy fandom, and then it popping. You know what I mean?

And then it's being over. Sure, I still get stopped for *Twilight* and stuff here and there. It was a reality check, and I'm so glad that I was surrounded by the right people. It was a reality check to where I realized, "That's not life. That's not going to last forever. You did *Twilight*, but you're not going to be offered the lead in the next Steven Spielberg movie." You know what I mean? That's just how it is.

Here I am auditioning again. I think having that done to me, and at the right age, was so awesome. I really appreciated that because it humbled me, and here I am. You still have to audition. I was so lucky to be a part of *X-Men*, and *Descendants* has been incredible. They will end. You know what I mean? 2015 was a slow year. Not a lot happened. I think things were just coming out for me. *Descendants* was getting released, and it's a year of publicity. In reality, I wasn't really working.

Bonnie: Publicity is a lot of work, but it doesn't generate a paycheck.

Booboo: It's not what I love to do. I feel like that's what I get paid to do. Being on sets is fun. It's such a weird thing. Something that has surprised me is just how humbling the industry can be inside of a world that's so, you know, boastful or arrogant, I guess. Overblown. But it is extremely humbling at the same time.

Dove Cameron

Dove: How second nature it was for me was very surprising because the industry is such a scary thing. "The industry"—it sounds like some kind of clan or something. It sounds like some kind of Dr. Who alien sect. I'm just surprised at how I've been able to adapt to it because from the outside it does sort of seem like this crazy, conspiracy theory world, when really it's just a bunch of crazy people. If you're crazy, you'll fit in just fine.

It surprised me that I haven't gone off some deep end. Everybody talks about "losing yourself to Hollywood," but I really feel like I haven't changed at all.

I definitely can't believe how many amazing incredible minds I've been able to meet through this. So many crazy artists, who are so brilliant. I guess I am surprised about that.

I'm surprised by so much. I'm surprised by how much I've learned about myself through being different people. That was always the reason I wanted to be an actor, was that self-exploration, and also understanding other people better. The practice of getting into the mind of someone who's not you, who hasn't shared your same experiences is so bettering for you as a person because then you do the same thing daily with people, walking around in the world. It makes you much more empathetic, sympathetic, thoughtful, and slower to react to things. It's like sharpening; your brain is a tool, and acting definitely sharpens your brain.

I think a lot of people do get lost in this industry when they make it about something other than bettering themselves and keeping a real eye on the fact that this isn't real life. If you keep your eyes open, if you look at yourself every day in the mirror and you still see that middle-school you, you keep in mind that this is a huge experience just like life is, and you keep one hand on your heart and one hand reaching out in front of you for anything that's trying to trip you up.

You focus on the good people that you meet, the smart people, the sweet people, the kind people, the people who are in it because they're artists and it's interesting to them, and it betters their relationship with themselves and other people; their family, their life, and their faith maybe even. Those people are in this industry, so that surprises me as well. People make it seem that Hollywood is full of snakes, and in the sense that everywhere is full of snakes, sure Hollywood has snakes in it, and so does any other place you're going to go. Any profession can have snakes in it, but don't let negative people deter you from being in this incredible industry.

You can have a real life in it, and I guess that's what I'm most surprised about. You can have a real life in something that is so malleable and ever changing. You can have a community, you can know yourself, and you can be stable. You don't have to be like what everybody says it's like in here. It's not really like that if you're not really like that.

Dylan Playfair

Dylan: Honestly, I just feel really fortunate. It worked quickly. It worked way faster than I thought it would. Very rarely do I come right out and say this, but I was geared up for four or five years of being in the trenches without roles because it was what I was exposed to when I was doing my research. Before I got into the industry, I had listened to so many actors talk about the years it took them to break the ice. I think coming in with that mentality of take your time, expect to work for years, expect it to be thankless and earn your way, and then when a year and a half later, I had done three movies and won a Leo award, wow, I really was surprised. It was something that I wasn't mentally prepared for.

I was loving that process. I was loving the process of, I don't need it tomorrow, and I can train for the next three years, and I'm just enjoying what I'm doing now. I think people can feel that and they can sense it when you don't have desperation in the room. Whether I knew it at the time or not, I think it really set me apart because I was really calm.

I was really calm about auditions. I was really calm about classes. I didn't have any anxiety of "When's it going to happen?" I know a lot of actors and actresses who have that anxiety and have that "I need to know soon, because if not, I need to do something else," whereas for me, I gave myself a window. It was long. It was five or six years before I was going to feel like "Okay, I got to start making cash in life."

I was totally prepared. I always reference hockey. I had broken down a four-year scholarship in my head, and then I had broken down the two extra years of junior hockey I would need to play to get that scholarship. For me, the other road was that long anyway before I would start making money playing hockey or having graduated out of university. That wasn't going to start until I was twenty-five anyhow. For me, I had bought myself five years of discovery time. I just so happened to have discovered acting, and it caught fire a lot faster than I thought it would.

Garrett Clayton

Garrett: I didn't know what kind of people I was going to meet when I moved here. It surprised me how long it took to find a group of people where I felt safe and that I trusted.

I think that's something that they don't tell you when you move here. There are a lot of people who don't always have the best intentions, who don't always want the best for you. They'll use you and whatever you have to get ahead. I was moving apartments once, and all of my things were stolen.

Another time I was moving, and the roommates I had didn't pay rent, but I had paid my portion of the rent, and the landlord said if they didn't pay, then they were going to put an eviction on all of our records. So I had to pay all of my money up front, and it was everything I had in my bank account, and then I found out they hadn't paid for a couple months. I just had to go back to the grind and get right back to work. That was when I was a waiter. Any money I'd saved, I was lucky to have. So, people can be very challenging here. I think you just have to be very meticulous and careful with whom you let in your life and who you trust, because it's very easy for people to want to get ahead and want to mislead when you first move out here.

Bonnie: I think one of the things that a lot of people who come to LA share is they've got this dream and a lot of ambition. Then the question is what kind of people are they? If they're good people, they're going to have that drive them in good ways that don't harm other people, but if their character isn't so strong, then they have no real problem stepping on other people to get to where they're trying to go. That's when you have to be really careful.

Garrett: Yeah. It just takes a long time to find people that you can really open up to and let care about you and you care about them. To invest in people is a very big deal out here. Any group of friends I've ever gotten to get close to is a very treasured thing in this city.

Jessica Marie Garcia

Jessica: In a weird way, it's surprised me and doesn't surprise me that I've actually done it. You know what I mean? It's so weird. I remember being in high school and being in a magnet program where everybody was actors. I didn't get cast in anything, nothing, my freshman year, my sophomore year. My junior year, seniors were casting things.

Then I got into stuff. Then I did *Who's Afraid of Virginia Woolf* in front of my director. At sixteen, doing my best job. I was so happy about it and being able to say, "No, you might not have cast me, but I did this," and people's entire perception of me changed. But they were still, "I'm going to college, I'm going to Dartmouth, and I'm going to NYU, and I'm going to be the best actor in New York," and I came out here, and nobody believed me.

They were all like, "You're going to go straight to LA? Good luck. You know the percentage of you making it." Now, I have all these friends that went to college. I'm not saying you shouldn't go to college by any means but just their attitudes toward it. Then they come here and want to do what I'm doing.

It takes a certain person. Harrison Ford said the only reason he made it is because he stood in line long enough, and I take that so to heart. He was a stand-in before he got...

Bonnie: He was a carpenter too, right?

Jessica: Harrison Ford is like Jesus. It's true, even on those days where I question myself so hard. There's a little part of me that is the biggest part of me that says. "Now, you got this." Even on those days where I think, "Oh god. I'm not good enough. I'm not pretty enough. I'm never going to be able to do these roles—I just say, "No, I will. If I have to write it myself, I will." That's inspiration from the fact that so many females against type are having their voices heard right now.

Bonnie: That's one of my favorite things—when there's a surprising casting choice and somebody shows up against type and blows everybody out of the water. It's thrilling.

Jessica: It's about time. I think Charlize Theron said something about how beautiful people have to fight for roles too because producers say, "Oh, you're too pretty for this role." I totally understand why people would be that way.

Bonnie: Look at her in *Monster*.

Jessica: Exactly. I was in *Monster*. It was the first movie I ever really did. I was an extra in the roller skating rink. It's so funny. I just remembered it. Seeing Patty Jenkins—oh my God, a female director blew my mind.

Sarah Jeffery

Sarah: It's not really all roses. It's not easy. It's not all glam and glitz. Like you said, it's not all red carpets, and it's not a cake walk. You really have to put your work into it. That's just something I've realized with time.

A surprise for me being young was you might meet people along the way who you don't jive with. There are a lot of bright personalities in this industry, and you have to focus on your own work, what works for you. It's definitely easy to get bothered by other people, but it's important to be in tune with your own morals and your own ethics.

Sometimes you might see things that are very uncomfortable for you. I've had some experiences on set with my early work, where as a young individual, I thought, "What? This isn't supposed to happen," but it can happen. As long as you stick to what you know and don't get sidetracked, you'll be okay. Having a support system is also a part of that.

Thomas Doherty

Thomas: The thing that surprised me the most is how underwhelming Hollywood is. Because you have all these notions of what Hollywood's going to be. You hear it in songs, and you see it in films. Now with the introduction of social media, you see it in pictures and videos. You see the cars and all the stuff. I guess as well, there's that sense of escapism, because there's something better than what you're already experiencing. What better place than Hollywood? What better? The glitz and the glam, the lights, and the superficiality of it all—the vacuous temple.

And it's not like that at all. So it's underwhelming in your expectations, but it's still incredible, from my experience anyway, because once you kind of get over that underwhelming sensation, you do realize that you have this fantastic blank canvas to work with. There's just all this possibility, which is amazing, but it's not the possibility that you thought it would be.

For some, I guess you could try and live up to your expectations of it. For me, living in that kind of vacuous perceived world that Hollywood is, is like sugar. It's that quick fix. Then you need sugar all the time, whereas, if you kind of see it for what it is, it's almost like brown rice. You can prolong the energy, and then your attention's not so much on the glitz and the glam, and the superficiality. Is that a word?

Bonnie: Yeah. Substance is available here.

Thomas: Substance is completely available. Yeah, that's a really good way of putting it. But it's not what you'd expect.

But it's fantastic. It really is, and it's amazing. It's really, really interesting. I guess the expectation of anything, in anyone's life, is kind of a destroyer of life.

Bonnie: Until you're in it, you just have this idea of it. The idea is never the same.

Thomas: It really isn't. So I think if you have your priorities straight as to why you want to do this, because for me...I liked acting, but I wanted to be famous. I was from Edinburgh, and I thought, "I want to be famous." Everyone says, "Oh, you're going to go to Hollywood." There's just this hype...Yeah, I wanted to be rich, and I wanted to be famous. Then you get a little taste of it, and it's just not what you thought it was going to be. You can live your life trying to fulfill this expectation, or you can see it for what it is and then go on a different route, which still involves being here, but it's not that vacuous way.

It's driven from a different place. So if you kind of get your desires, what you actually want from this place, it's an incredible hub of activity. You can just flourish, and you can do so much. That's only if your priorities are kind of right. If they're on the purity of acting and working with actors, amazing actors, for their acting abilities, and not for their fame, it's incredible.

I think if you come here in pursuit of fame and fortune, you're going to be underwhelmed, and you're also going to be exhausted trying to chase this illusion.

Bonnie: I think your analogy of sugar is really good, because it does give you this quick sort of fix, if you will.

Thomas: Yeah, it's unsustainable.

Victoria Moroles

Victoria: A lot of people do think it's a lot of glitz and glamor, and it's not. I think once I started heavily working consistently, the surprise was that it's something completely different than I had ever imagined.

Yes, I think it's glitz and glamor, but in a different way. It's raw; it's hard. If you really dedicate yourself to it, it's draining. That was probably the biggest aha moment that I had when I realized what I had gotten myself into and realized, "You want to do this for the rest of your life? Okay. That's going to take some time to get used to, and to accustom your thought process of what you thought it was going to be, to what the reality of it is. Do you love that?" I do, but some people might not. You always have to keep an open mind whenever you are going in there because you might have the idea of what it might be, and it might not be that.

Bonnie: I think for most people it can't be, because it's just its own thing, but it's so different than what it looks like. I remember talking to your mom, and there was a period of time where you were a recurring guest star on two different shows, both *Liv and Maddie* and *Teen Wolf.* They were both writing stuff for you, and you were shooting them back to back on the same day, basically night and day for a while. That must have been intense.

Victoria: It was so intense. I know there was a good week where I was probably getting four hours of sleep or just napping wherever I could. I love that. I love being busy. It makes me happy, but you really have to stay grounded and stay healthy because, I would go at 8:00 a.m. to *Liv and Maddie*. We'd do rehearsal and whatever. I'd get off in the afternoon, go straight to *Teen Wolf*, and we'd shoot till two in the morning, and then I had to get up and go… It's really physically taxing and mentally taxing.

Bonnie: It's a good problem to have, but it's not for the faint of heart.

Victoria: Yeah. No, of course not, but it's fun. I love it. It's good.

Luke Benward

Luke: A surprise was when I had turned nineteen and moved out.

Bonnie: Out of your parents' house.

Luke: Yeah, exactly, and realized how hard this business actually is, honestly. That was more of a wake up call. I was always under their shelter, under their protection, and they shielded their boy from the storm. I moved out of their house, got a couple roommates, and started doing it on my own. It took a moment to get used to the cold water. I had my little development moment. Really, some hard nights of, "What am I doing? Am I good enough?" The normal things everyone goes through.

I came through it, and I feel like that one brought me in touch with myself much better but also gave me a confidence, in not me as an actor, but me as an artist, me as somebody who's going to create something and who has something to bring to the table, which is really what I am as an actor. I'm here to create, and if I'm true to myself, I feel like I'm being true to the art I'm supposed to be putting out there.

Bonnie: I love that. I think that's beautiful, and it's very true. Look, there's that incredibly challenging transition when you leave your parents house whether you're eighteen, nineteen, twenty, whatever. A lot of kids go off to college, and some kids just move out and start making it on their own. That's got a lot of moments of truth in it, if you're aware. If you're an artist, you're sort of extra aware.

Luke: Definitely. Acting is awesome when you're on set, but when you're not, it's just a constant job search. Always. The odds are ever stacked against you. I didn't really like to go out and meet people, I guess, when I was living at home, but I started to go out more and network, and I hate it. You meet a lot of people who are doing the same thing you are. Good looking, better looking, the best looking, talented, not talented. There are just a lot of people. It can be frustrating for sure.

You have to find the constants. There are some things in people's lives that don't change, you know, that are rock steady. For me, it is my family and myself as a creator. The confidence comes, really, from the things that I know are supporting me.

Cameron Boyce

Cameron: I think the thing that surprises me the most...I've never really gotten used to the impact that I've had on people. When I walk out of my house, I still feel like nobody's going to recognize me. I still do that. And people do recognize me, and sometimes I hear these stories about, "Oh my gosh, I was going through a really tough time this past week, and I turned on an episode of *Jessie* and you were really funny, and you brought me joy when I needed it and thank you."

I don't really think about that because I like to sort of return to normal life when I leave set, when I can. But when I hear stories like that, all I can think is, "Wow, that's really cool."

A lot of people do things, and they don't really think about the kind of effect it has. But my butterfly effect is really broad. I reach a lot of people in a lot of different parts of the world. And my world is very small. I have a very selective group of friends, and I don't really hang out with a whole bunch of people. I don't do a lot of partying or anything like that. I'm sort of a homebody. But my work reaches a lot of places, and it affects a lot of people. And that's something that I still can't fully wrap my head around, and maybe it's better that I can't wrap my head around it because the weight of that is really heavy.

But I've read things, I've seen things on Instagram where people say, "I'm really, really having a difficult time, but your performance in this show or this movie has inspired me to keep going."

I literally just sent a direct message to a girl who was talking about how she doesn't feel like she has a purpose, and I just said, "You do have a purpose, and I just want you to know that I'm here for you, and all of the people who support me will support you. Just remember that." I just sort of threw that out there. And I had never talked to this person before. And her username was "Cameron's-something." And what it meant to her...you can't even imagine. And it took me three seconds to type it. And I meant every word that I said, but it was so easy for me to just reach out for two seconds and say, "Hey, you matter. I care about you. Thank you for your support. I'm going to support you back." And what it meant to her was insane. She was over the moon about it.

People ask me all the time, "Does it ever get annoying when people ask for pictures?" No. It takes two seconds to take a picture. Does it get dangerous sometimes? Sure. Sometimes you have to move on. Sometimes you can't stay in one place.

Bonnie: And that's a safety thing for everybody, not just you.

Cameron: Seriously. And some days we're tired; some days we can't handle it. But if I saw someone that I really admired, I would want a picture; I would want to talk to them for a second. So that's the thing. You've just got to look at it from the other person's perspective. And that goes for a lot of things. Just look at it from the other person's perspective, and you'll get a better understanding of them and yourself.

And that's one of our responsibilities. We chose that, you know? We chose this life. We chose to be the kid on TV. And we enjoy every second of it. So what comes with that is what comes with that. And you can't turn your back on that; the people who support you, who keep you on the air. You've got to let them know that you appreciate them. But it really surprises me, talking about the question again, just the kind of impact that you have on people and how it means so much to just, in two seconds, take a quick picture. I put my arm around somebody, I smile, and that gets them through the rest of their week. It's crazy.

Bonnie: It's beautiful to be able to make that kind of a difference.

Cameron: It's insane. And you get jaded a little bit. There are times where you think, I'm just taking pictures. But certain people remind you. Like hey, listen, you mean a lot to my life. And that's when you sit back and go, "Dang, I did something really good apparently. I was just doing my job." But it means a lot to people. So that will always, for the rest of time, probably, surprise me.

10

The Disney Channel

IT'S THE DREAM of millions to be on the Disney Channel. These young artists have had that dream come true. What was it like?

Every actor on the Disney Channel began as a professional working actor. They trained and auditioned, in many cases, for years before one day, one of those auditions landed them a role with Disney. Almost every actor known for their work on the Disney Channel experienced being rejected by Disney multiple times before all the stars aligned.

And while working for Disney can feel magical, it is also genuinely work. Disney, in particular, has such a large reach because its actors spend a lot of time doing promotional work of one kind or another, outside of actually filming their film or TV roles. Promotional work can be like a second job.

Disney casts some actors through nationwide or even international searches, and they have discovered others through huge general auditions. Most young actors who are cast in series regular roles on their TV shows live in the Los Angeles area, have an agent, and begin with a role or two as a guest star on a Disney Channel show before being considered for something bigger.

While Disney doesn't require their talent to be triple threats that can act, sing, and dance, it does help! And you may be surprised to know that all the young actors are older than the characters they play...sometimes well into their twenties. So if it's your dream to be on the Disney Channel, read on, and learn about the experience of these young artists.

Dove Cameron

Dove: I wanted to be on Disney so bad when I was younger. I think it's kind of a rite of passage. Not every kid—I don't want to pigeonhole you, I don't know who I'm talking to—but I definitely did. And you better believe that I don't forget that I'm still living out my childhood dream. I don't ever wake up and think, "Ugh, time to go to my boring job." I love Disney. I love the company. I love the people I work for. I love what I do with my days. They are definitely very long days.

What I have to tell you is that Disney Channel is a channel, is potentially whatever you would do with them, is a TV show, is a movie, is a movie franchise, is whatever. It's a huge company. You have to know if you want to work for Disney, it's not just something that you do lightly. It takes up a lot of time. I don't think people really realize that. When you're not shooting, you're doing the promotions, the advertising, the interstitials, the interviews, the music videos, and everything else. That's why it has such incredible exposure. It's because they generate more content than anybody else. It's the best life that you can sign on for, if that's what you want.

If you also want to be doing other things or you want to be going to school or you want a slower start, it's definitely something you have to know what you're getting into. The company has always treated me incredibly well. They really do treat you like family, but it is long hours. If you're interested in signing on for that, now that I have told you...they sometimes have really big casting calls. Disney is great that way where they will go to some big cities, and you can drive to those. They have those every once in awhile where they do huge cattle calls. I would just say for those, you'd better stay on top of it and be one of the first in line because there are so many people there. I don't know if they get to everybody.

Bonnie: I have a link on my website on the "Resources" page for where you can find the one legitimate source for the opportunities to audition for Disney even if you don't have an agent. Here is the link to that page: https://bonniejwallace.com/resources-for-actors/.

Dove: Awesome! Yeah, so go check that out, you guys.

Disney, like I said, generates a lot of content, so they're constantly auditioning for new projects. Click on that website, the website that is verified, on my mom's page. Also, if you already have an agent, tell them that you want to go for Disney Channel. They probably already have their finger on the pulse of that, because they are always looking for new talent, new bright faces, and I could not speak more to the generosity and good quality of the company. If you want that start, if you want that huge kick start, that sort of nose to the grindstone, four years of education in the industry, I could not recommend them more. It's the best job in the world if that's what you want.

Brenna D'Amico

Bonnie: In my experience with all the actors that I know who've been on the Channel, they first fell in love with acting. In many cases, it was musical theater. So many of you guys are triple threats.

Yet, to be a professional actor is literally to go out for whatever you're called out to do. It can be any project at all, and it's completely random. It's so random it's kind of mind-blowing sometimes. You know, it's a horror film today. Then it's a commercial tomorrow, or whatever. Then one day for each of you, it happens to be the Disney Channel.

I think there's a lot of confusion out there by non-actors thinking, "I want to be a Disney Channel actor." It doesn't work that way. You're an actor, and then maybe you get an audition that maybe turns into a role. And here you are, and you're doing all this work on the Disney Channel. What's that been like?

Brenna: It's still surreal for me, because I always watched *Hannah Montana, Lizzie McGuire*. I watched *Wizards of Waverly Place*. So many different ones—*High School Musical*. I had the Hannah Montana microphone and everything, so just seeing and knowing that I'm on Disney Channel is still so surreal and crazy for me to think about, and I'm so grateful that that happened for me.

I didn't go into acting thinking of a particular production or channel that I wanted to be on. I just knew I wanted to act, so when I got that audition for Disney, I was like, "This is so exciting. This is so cool that I actually get to audition for them."

I didn't do voice-over before *Wicked World*, and I fell in love with it. I absolutely fell in love with it. Voice acting has been another growing passion of mine, and I've been getting a lot of auditions for it, which I'm so grateful for. Just the different voices that I found out I could do was so liberating to find out and experience. I love voice acting; I really, really do, and it's another one of my passions.

Bonnie: The same thing happened with Dove. It just wasn't really on her radar. Then some opportunities came up, because the way that seems to work is one opportunity leads to other opportunities. She loves it too. I think it's just a really fun thing that a lot of actors don't think about.

Brenna: Right, they don't think about it. I don't think people understand how fun and creative it is. You can do so much with it. What they do in auditions—or when you do get a show—is they have you say it three different ways. It's so fun experimenting and coming up with those three different ways to say it.

I really love it because you can do so much with it on your own. It's what you want to do. Same thing with acting, I just love that you can take control and figure out what you want to do with the characters.

Bonnie: I love that too, and if you're lucky, you'll have a director who supports that kind of fluidity.

Brenna: Yeah, and Kenny (Ortega) does that.

Kenny is so amazing. His energy vibrates off of him and just makes everybody so comfortable. The energy he exudes is positivity and happiness and excitement. That type of energy is so amazing to feel yourself. He lets everybody explore what they want to do, and I think that's amazing.

Booboo Stewart

Booboo: It was interesting. I've had an odd relationship with Disney. I started doing music for them and that was that. I just did music for them. Acting-wise, Disney has always been really difficult for me. Really, really hard. It's a different kind of acting. I've always come from—I don't want to say a movie background—just a different background. You know what I mean? When you're doing Disney, I feel it's closer to doing stage work, and I've never done stage. I've never been a loud person. When I did Disney auditions, they've been, "Okay, again but just more energy. Louder. Bigger."

And I was like, "Okay." Here we go. And it's always been bad. There's a fine line of doing Disney work and different work. I think so. I respect Disney. Like Dove being on a Disney show all that time; that's a lot of work, and it's a lot of energy, and it's very difficult. My hat goes off to all of the Disney actors because I would never get any of the parts. I auditioned and auditioned. That twenty-first floor in the Disney Building.

I was there so many times but never booked anything until I did a few guest spots on *Good Luck Charlie*. I did two guest spots on that, and I did a thing on *Kickin' It* because I did martial arts and I knew Leo and...

It was one of those things. I probably wouldn't have got the part. Then *Descendants*. Since then, *Lab Rats*. I did a few. I played a villain on that show, which was kind of fun.

Now my hat goes off to Disney and all of the actors that have ever been a part of Disney. It's very difficult, and it takes a lot of work.

Bonnie: Now you're warming up to go film *Descendants 2*?

Booboo: Yeah, *Descendants 2*, which I feel is a happy medium. It's interesting. The first one, Dove helped me immensely to get that part because one, going into those auditions I was extremely nervous. And two, I just had no idea what level to play it, because, again, I had never done anything for Disney, so I'm like, "Do I be really big and crazy, or do I…" This is a movie with Kenny directing it. You know *High School Musical* wasn't crazy over the top. I mean, certain characters were escalated, but Zack wasn't. He played it pretty cool, and Vanessa played it pretty cool, so it's kind of confusing where to be. I just remember Dove and I going into a different room, and she just loosened me up and got me into the spirit of what it was. I thought, "Okay. All right. I think I can do it."

Jessica Marie Garcia

Jessica: I think that I owe my career to the Disney Channel honestly. Everything I've worked on has been a platform of Disney. *The Middle* is ABC and before that I did *Huge*, which was ABC Family before, now Freeform. If it wasn't for those casting directors and those networks that said yes…

Suzanne Goddard-Smythe and then G. Charles Wright, if it wasn't for them, I just would not be here, and I don't even think that I would continue to have a career right now. I owe everything to the Disney Channel. The fact that they weren't looking for a Hispanic, crazy, weirdo person, like me, even for this role. Their platform is ridiculous. It's huge, and I think that they take it so seriously.

They're so specific about the content that they give and the message that they give out. I think we're lucky. I grew up watching Disney Channel. *Lizzie McGuire* was my everything. *That's So Raven*. I dreamed of being on Disney Channel. The fact that I am is insane. The fact that I'm a part of Disney history is my pride and joy right now. Insane.

Sarah Jeffery

Sarah: It's been so fun. It's been a breath of fresh air, going from these incredibly dramatic emotional parts, which are rewarding in their own way, to getting to have a lot of fun while working very hard. It's been amazing. *Descendants* was such an amazing experience. You were there for it all. It was literally magical. That's a part of me forever. Additionally, all the things that have come with it: getting to see my own doll.

It's absolutely mind-blowing. Insane. I walk into Target and think, "What?"

It's crazy. It's really a sweet experience. I've made friends that I will have for the rest of my life. It's the best. I get to do what I love, and I get to meet incredible people.

Bonnie: Then it led to some really cool voice work with the *Wicked World* shorts, which are so cool and fun.

Sarah: So fun. I had the most fun doing voice-overs for that. It's so cool. I've done a dance along for it, which is so fun, just really lighthearted fun things. That being said, it's work. Finding your character, staying committed uses a lot of energy.

Bonnie: Your dance training was probably an integral part of your getting that role.

Sarah: Yeah, it was. I won't lie, I auditioned many times for the part of Audrey. I went back and I went back, but thankfully Kenny was a big advocate for me, Kenny and Wendy— Kenny the director, and Wendy was one of the producers.

Bonnie: Kenny Ortega and Wendy Japhet.

Sarah: Yes. They were big advocates for me and said, "We want you to get this part, so we're going to work with you until we get just the sweet spot," and we found the part, and it was a collaboration, and it's been one of the most rewarding auditioning experiences I've ever had.

Garrett Clayton

Garrett: I'd always wanted to be on it when I was a kid, so for me, it was exciting. I finally got to be on that thing that I'd idolized growing up. I started when I was in my early twenties.

Bonnie: You're not alone. There are a lot of people in their twenties on the channel.

Garrett: Which I didn't even realize at the time. I kept thinking, "They're never going to cast me." I'm twenty. It was great. It was fun. I also know I got very lucky because for *Teen Beach Movie*, they flew us to Puerto Rico. We got to go, literally, film a movie on an island where people vacation. I got to live there for months.

It was just such an extravagant production. It was a wonderful magical...You know, I got to risk everything moving to LA, and then I get to go to this...It felt very old Hollywood...Just everything about it. There's a song called "Surf Crazy" in the first movie, and it's my character's big number, and it's the first real musical number of the movie, and they wanted to make it really grand, so they had this big crane while they were going and shooting. I remember being on the beach and just getting to sing and...you get really close with all the dancers on the movie, when you're doing musicals, and getting to be surrounded by friends and getting to have this moment, getting to be on the channel that I idolized for years. It was very surreal. It felt very old Hollywood.

Luke Benward

Luke: I'm forever thankful to Disney. I mean—they gave me work for years. They gave me a platform where I could safely explore as a child. They're, as you could assume, great with families. That's who they cater to, and they cater to children. They obviously are great with children, and I had nothing but phenomenal experiences with Disney. The executives were always so kind to me. They sent me birthday and Christmas presents...They'd reach out and encourage me. Yeah, I'm forever thankful to Disney. I wouldn't have had nearly the résumé and had nearly the work and the avenues in which to continue acting if it wasn't for them.

I love what they continue to do. Put out art for kids. Good, wholesome shows for children.

And shows that teach children to have good morals. Everyone always kind of brings it back to that Disney has a cheesy thing where it's like they get in a fight, and at the end of the episode, they sit down and have a heart to heart. And it is cheesy, but I think it's a really great thing to teach kids because communication is so important, and I've noticed a lot of people in my generation have trouble communicating. They get angsty or they get shut down or they just...I guess because of phones and being online and that kind of stuff, it's disconnected.

I love that Disney has continued to have rich stories and morals in all their shows, really.

Bonnie: I'm with you. A lot of those projects are a lot of fun too.

Luke: Are they ever a blast! *Cloud 9* was so fun. Yeah. It was freezing, and we worked our tails off. It was definitely a fun experience. They put a bunch of young kids up in the snow in the mountains.

Bonnie: It was like summer camp in the snow, with really long hours.

Luke: Exactly, yeah.

Victoria Moroles

Victoria: It was my high school experience, because I was supposed to be going through high school during that time in my life. That's why it was like that for me. I loved working for Disney. I loved going and filming *Cloud 9*, because I met so many amazing people. It was a really cool place to film, and it was fun. Having done *Teen Wolf* and then also this thriller, it's completely different from where I started out.

I think about it all the time, how much I miss multicam and how much I miss comedy and how much I miss kids and living in the kid world. I love that. One of my favorite things was doing live tapings and getting to be at a full contact with the kids. I love kids. That was a blast for me.

It is really different, and that comes with the territory of Disney Channel. Disney Channel is its own genre obviously. When I first started out, I wasn't too good at multicam or anything, but once I started working on *Liv and Maddie*, you kind of just get in the groove. You get in the groove of it. I had never done theater but going every day and then rehearsing, and then filming the two days, even if you do the live show, it feels like so much more of a production. It's quick, and it's upbeat, and it's happy, and you are living in this wonderful happy headspace all the time. You just get to be a big kid, and I loved it. I think about it all the time.

Bonnie: That was a really special group of people too.

Victoria: Yeah, most definitely. I'm just very lucky to have been a part of that group. It was really awesome.

Joey Bragg

Joey: They were the first people I auditioned for. I would go
         and do auditions for them constantly. I would drive down
         from the Bay Area, five hours each way and auditioned
         for the brother in *Dog with a Blog* and all these differ-
         ent pilots, and my first pilot I booked was a Disney XD
         show called *Gulliver Quinn* with Jon Heder. In the audi-
         tion process, I would do stand-up for them...If you're a
         singer on Disney Channel, they have you sing. I did stand-
         up for them. They liked it. I got cast in this pilot. I left high
         school as a sophomore to film this pilot, and they were
         like, "This is the best pilot we've ever shot; we love it. Jon
         Heder from *Napoleon Dynamite* is the star. Of course, it's
         going to get picked up." I spent six months going back to
         school after filming this pilot, doing stand-up regularly,
         thinking, "This is going to happen; I've got to start pre-
         paring for this."

         Obviously it didn't happen, but I was so young, and it was
         one of my first things, and it was just not what I enjoyed.
         I don't like sitting around and waiting for a call. I like to be
         proactive and doing what I want to be doing. I had a blast
         shooting the pilot. It was fun.

         Then I auditioned for other things. They just kept bring-
         ing me in, and there were certain roles where they would
         change it to be like me, and there was a character in this
         pilot that was changed to be a stand-up, and they were
         going to make it the lead, and then things happened,
         and that changed. Then I was going to be the friend that
         wanted to do stand-up...I didn't want another six months
         of waiting for a pilot to get picked up. Just that feeling,
         it just wasn't fun...I don't like anxiety. I don't feel anxiety

about anything, but just putting my faith in someone else doing something for me…

It was absolutely out of my hands, and it was nothing I could have worked for. It was nothing I really could have done, so I turned that pilot down and said I didn't want to do it. Then they moved on, and I was brought in for a couple other things, and then *Bits and Pieces* came along *(Liv and Maddie)*, and I went in and I auditioned for it, and I think I had an initial audition where I met with John and Ron, and the producers and the casting director, and then they brought me in to do it in front of network. I did it in front of network, and before chemistry tests or any kind of tests, they have you sign a contract. I didn't want to do it.

It wasn't about the money. It was about the six months of sitting there on my butt, waiting for them to call.

Bonnie: Apparently, Disney Channel takes longer than almost anybody to make that decision. You can't take on any other potentially conflicting projects for that amount of time. You're basically on hold.

Joey: Finally, two months go by, and then I get a call about them coming back with three months exclusivity, my stand-up was void, anything I write was voided in the contract, and just basically I could do whatever I wanted, but also I was going to be on this Disney Channel show, so then I said, "Yeah, that's exactly what I wanted to do." Three months of not doing anything else after we shoot the pilot.

Bonnie: That's more normal.

Joey: Three months. I did it obviously, and the last day of my three-month hold, they called me, and then I got the script, and the character's name was Joey. And it was perfect, and it was great, and then I had the best four years of my life filming that show.

Bonnie: That was a special show. It was our first big experience too. When it's your first experience, you don't have a lot to compare it with. How can you know it's not always like that? To have so many people on the show who were career writers and grips and electricians and hair and makeup people and wardrobe and everybody else say, "This is the best show I've ever worked on." It was amazing.

Joey: It's also amazing too, because I was working with people that believed in me and were big fans of what I was already doing, and there were certain things like—when I talk about opportunities that I've passed up or just been too lazy and not taking advantage of completely—I probably could have written an episode had I not been a lazy sixteen-year-old kid. Or I probably should have been doing stand-up and not let that fall through the cracks and just done both.

There's a lot of things that I would have done differently, and I think that, in the future, all that did was teach me what I'm going to do differently. I'm so happy that it happened at such a young age because everything's happened for me at such a young age.

I have just been so incredibly lucky that even if nothing happens, I'm just happy with what I've done because this is such a business where you never know what's going to happen. Again, I don't think I'll ever find what I think of as success because I don't know what success is. I've never felt content with where I am in my career, but it was an amazing, amazing start. A lot of people think that a Disney Channel show is the roller coaster that's going to take you on to the rest of your career, but in real life, it's more of a diving board that just gets you up. It gets you an amazing social media following, which now is going to have an everlasting effect on whether or not I get cast in things, and you've just got to find your way from there as opposed to hoping that that shows you your way.

Bonnie: To me, I always think of it as an extraordinary spring-board. It's really the same metaphor because it gets you up, but then what do you do with it? Part of that's up to you. Part of that's luck. It's amazing thing to have that kind of platform because nobody builds a platform like they do.

Joey: They're amazing.

11

What's Important for Success

THERE IS NOTHING like experiencing a high level of success to help you get clear on what really is and is not important for success.

These artists may be young, but they have already achieved enough of their dreams to see very clearly through the illusions that fame and money can create.

What do these young stars value? What do they feel is genuinely important for success? Here are a few highlights:

- Stability
- Being well regarded by peers for their kindness and work ethic
- Being true to yourself
- Making art that impacts others
- Having a strong family life and personal relationships
- Feeling happy and peaceful
- Doing projects you enjoy
- Enjoying the people you work with
- Believing in yourself
- Believing that what you want to do is worth doing
- Having friends you can trust

- Letting go of perfectionism
- Cultivating an ability to stay present
- Cultivating gratitude
- Realizing that success and happiness are two different things

It's interesting to see what is not on this list: there are no mentions of material things like expensive clothes, cars, or houses.

What you see mentioned consistently: being true to yourself, feeling happy, having strong relationships, coming from a place of gratitude, and being part of a team.

Read on for some inspiration and brilliant life advice...

Dove Cameron

Dove: I'm totally stealing this from the documentary *Happy*, and if you haven't seen it, you have to watch it, and I'm not going to fully do it justice, but *not* important is fame, money, and popularity. If you are in this industry because you think it's going to fill some hole in you, or you want to make money, or you want to be on a private jet or be on a yacht with a model, or whatever, there are people who are doing that, and I cannot speak to their quality of life.

For me, if I look at myself as a measure of success, which I do, I feel very successful. Not in a cocky way, in a sense of like "I'm so successful, I'm so famous, I'm like Cher or Britney, or whatever." I'm not at all. I'm not like anybody in the same way that you're not like anybody. I'm not the most famous, the most rich, or the highest on IMDb. I'm not, and I may not ever be; that's not what I'm aiming for, and it's not what I was ever aiming for.

My measure of success is stability. You spend a large percentage of your time working, because obviously, that is a measure of success when people want to work with you. A huge measure of success for me is when I walk away from a project and people speak well of me. When they say I genuinely want to work with you again, I suggested you to this person, and I just think that you are very kind, you're very hard working, you mean well, and you have a good conscience.

That's a huge measure of success for me. When somebody comes up to me and says, "You know I was just talking to this person last week, and they said you are such a good person, a hard worker, and you lead that set well." That's my biggest measure of success: when I leave a project well. When I leave it better than when I started, and I've only ever worked with actors who are the same way.

It is a big team effort. To me one of the biggest measures of success is when you treat those around you, who you work with, well. From the grips to the director, to props, set dec, and actors, everybody.

Luke Benward

Luke: I've been trying to just not think about success. I'm working right now with Melissa McCarthy and going into it, I didn't really know what to expect. I hadn't met her before, except for one time in our chemistry read. She's obviously a very successful and famous comedian. She's incredible. Immediately I got on the set and felt so welcomed by her and her husband, who is directing the film. They're extremely successful, and she is incredible to work with, so smart, but on camera she really just creates. Whatever comes out, she just commits, and that is the moment. Whatever comes out, that is what the scene is about. She's amazing.

I want to say this is the most enjoyable set I've ever been on. Everyone is just so much a team, and helping each other out. There's no stress because everyone's just doing their stuff, and it's really been amazing and really a great environment to create in. I guess I look at all the successful people, and they don't care is one thing I've started to realize. They kind of walk to the beat of their own drum. They're true to themselves.

When you hear art, and you see art where you feel "That impacts me because of how much it impacted them," I think that is true of success. When someone can look at this creator and say, "Whoa, I'm going to have to take a beat and kind of digest what I just saw because they were feeling those emotions." You know what I mean?

That feeling of "I need to take a step back," that, in my mind, is what I think of when I think of success.

Bonnie: That's beautiful. That's artistic success, and you were speaking just before that about hanging on to the things that don't change no matter what, like your family. These things that transcend fortunes of one kind or another is another thing that I know is important to you because I know family is very important to you.

Luke: Definitely. I mean, just to use Melissa as an example, when I look at her, I see a husband, a phenomenal marriage, and they love each other, and they support each other. I see two beautiful little girls who are on set and talking to mommy and daddy. I see that infrastructure as well, which is another kind of evidence of success.

Sarah Jeffery

Sarah: I think, for me, a large part of it has been finding myself as an actor and not striving to be someone else.

That said, I think it's also important to learn from other people and continue to find inspiration from your fellow actors, and from any art, whatever it may be. Staying true to yourself and finding what makes you unique, that's important for me.

Bonnie: That's huge. I think a lot of people go in basically trying to do what they think is expected of them, fit in that shape that is offered to them, or that the shape they think that they're supposed to fit into, and they kind of bend themselves into a pretzel that's really unnatural. You can't succeed if you do that, because you can't sustain it.

Sarah: Trying to cultivate your own image is important. I think social media is incredible for some things, but it's also easy to look at other young actors or whoever and think, "They're successful. That means I have to be exactly what they are."

Bonnie: Right, and emulate them in all the wrong ways.

Sarah: Exactly. That's a big thing for me, recognizing where it's good to draw inspiration and where you need to stay true to yourself.

Thomas Doherty

Thomas:　I guess there are different layers of that question. What's ultimate success?

I guess the ultimate success is happiness; contentment, peace, joy—that's almost the ultimate. You could argue and say, "No, but my ultimate success is to be a famous actor with a Ferrari." But in being a famous actor, and having that Ferrari, that's going to make you happy.

Or you think it might make you happy. I think the ultimate success is to be happy. Once I kind of understood that fame, fortune cannot make you happy, because you experience happiness inside of yourself...if you're unhappy, no amount of money or cars can make you happy, can't do it. So I think if your priority is happiness with understanding that fame and fortune cannot make you happy, it's fun; enjoy it, of course. But it's not going to make you happy.

That's the ultimate success, for me: to be peaceful, to be joyful, to be happy, to be content. Then when you're in that state, you're more productive in what you're passionate about. So you've got more energy, you've got more enthusiasm...You've just got more lust for life when you're in that frame of mind. Then everything's a possibility. Then everything is an open book. Then everything is an opportunity. If you channel that into acting, specifically, not exclusively, then you're going to flourish.

Dylan Playfair

Dylan: For me, it's doing projects that you like doing. It's funny because you hear really successful actors being asked, "What brought you to the role? What attracted you to the role?" The truth of it is I just audition for everything, praying to God that any one of them work.

It's the one that wanted me, and I said yes, and I was available for it. There's definitely a force that we don't really have a say in, and I think as far as when these projects come your way and why you're right for them at that moment in time...I did three projects that required hockey players. If that's not the universe saying you've done it at the right time, I don't know what is.

Who knows? Maybe if I had waited four years or five years, there would have been projects that came in that needed not a hockey player but someone else in a world that I understood. I think for me it was finding projects and finding people within those projects that were in the same headspace I was. There are a lot of people who are really passionate about film, and I think there are a lot of people who are less passionate.

I think to find the ones who you share values with and to make projects with those kinds of people, that's going to give you a fulfilling feeling. *Letterkenny* is a show that I make with my friends. We started out on YouTube, and we're going into our third season now. We've had a huge amount of success in Canada, and these guys are guys that I was hanging out with on weekends playing B league with anyway. To go into the other sets that I've been fortunate to be a part of, I really haven't had a group of bad apples. The reason why I say there are those guys out there who aren't passionate is because I've heard horror stories of other actors who've dealt with people who don't want to be there, and I've been lucky. Every show I've been on, people have had fun. I think that's important. To have fun in what you're doing.

It's a job that's really unlike other jobs where you have to be enjoying it, even the difficult scenes, even the hard projects. You've got to want to go to work in the morning. You've got to want to work twenty-hour days with people. You've got to build a team mentality around that project and have everyone pushing the same or pulling the same direction. All the projects I've done, we've had that feeling on set. I think that spills over. It's a really small world too. People know pretty much everyone else in the industry within a couple of projects. It's weird how small this world becomes.

Bonnie: Everybody is one degree of separation away from everybody else, pretty much.

Dylan: People talk. If you are that guy who has that good vibe on set, you want to be around that. I think that's played a huge part in working with similar people repeatedly and being asked to come back. I love what I'm doing. I really do. I really enjoy it.

Joey Bragg

Joey: One thing that was said to me when I was a little kid is that you can get anywhere with confidence and a clipboard.

You can walk behind the scenes at Safeway or Vons or whatever, and if you're walking around acting like you're not supposed to be there, someone will kick you out, but if you walk around acting like you're supposed to be there, then you're supposed to be there.

That's something that goes with this business. If you always feel like you should be where you are, then you're going to belong where you are. I know that counteracts a lot of what I've said earlier, but if you just believe in yourself and who you want to be, and that what you want to be doing is worth doing, then that's what success is.

Booboo Stewart

Booboo: You grow up in your family, and they always tell you this, but having a solid group of people around you, people you can trust, even your friend group—like just start with your friend group, literally. Especially once things start picking up.

Having the right friends. I've had the same friends, literally, for such a long time. My best friends are the same three guys, four guys. You know what I mean? I think that that is something I really value. Being able to call my friends and talk and just vent. I know that they won't go telling other people, and I know that the advice they give me is honest advice.

Sometimes too honest. Like, I didn't need to hear that. You know, that part of the movie—okay, I didn't need to hear that. I really think that honest people, you know, good friends, family, that's such an important thing. Because the more success you have, the more random hangers-on, like "Who is this guy?" "Why do you keep texting me?" You want to be my friend too much. It's weird.

Bonnie: "And I don't even really know you."

Booboo: Exactly. It's like, "Why do you want to be my friend? We've never even talked." It's a weird thing.

I think for me, as far as work goes, being less stressed just in daily life. When you have a meeting, when you have an audition, just don't sweat the little things. It doesn't matter. Life goes on. Just let it happen. I used to want to be perfect, like you've got to be perfect in everything you do, but you don't have to be. Imperfection is fantastic for our line of work, I think. Who wants to watch a perfect person on TV?

Bonnie: I love that because a lot of artists have perfectionist tendencies.

Booboo: And I do. I'm not saying I don't. My friend, Ben, what does he call it? It's called PTT or something like that. Post-take trauma. PTT, yeah. It's after you do a scene. You start saying it, and after you've got it, like in your head…I don't know…all the ways you could have done it. Stop sweating the little things. You know what I mean? Just stop. If you trust your director, it's in their hands now. You don't have to be the perfectionist.

Bonnie: I think that so many of you guys are so accomplished in part because you have such high standards. You hold yourself to a really high standard, but you're learning as you go that you actually do better as a human being and probably also as an artist if you find ways to just...let that go.

Booboo: Yeah, 100 percent, you've got to just let it go.

Victoria Moroles

Victoria: I've been thinking a lot about that lately. I think what's really important is that you create a life outside of your job, and you focus on all the other aspects of your life, because if you pour yourself into this and you forget about putting your energy into all those other things, it'll come back to you.

Balance has really been a huge focus of mine. Staying present, completely present, because you can't worry too much about what you are going to do in the future or what's going to be next, especially in this industry. Inconsistency is the name of the game. If you don't like inconsistency, which I don't—I'm a very consistent person; I'm a very structured person—then it can be really hard.

I think, especially this year, being present was a really big thing for me, because you can have all the success in the world but...like, when I booked the film. You think when I book that film, I'll be happy. When I do this, it'll be perfect. You know what? You can't think about it like that, because it could be that way, but you are just going to end up letting yourself down, and the other parts of you will kind of blow away. Especially in this industry, it's important to keep your mind and your body healthy, because that is your tool.

I guess my biggest thing is to keep your mind, your body and your soul happy 100 percent so that you can work and focus on the other successes of life that you can have. Focus on family is huge for me. After I did the movie, I took a month off, and I spent the entire leave with my family. Whatever is important to you, just keep that in mind. Of course it's really good to work at a new job, every single day and stuff, but you should also keep all the other things intact.

Bonnie: Yes, because the truth is the work is not always going to be there. If you keep investing in your friends and in your family, so that your relationships are always there for you, that's part of what makes your life worth living and keeps you afloat in between.

Victoria: As an actor, it's our job to story tell. It's our job to live the lives of other people. How can we do that if the only life we live is an actor? Yes, we have to study our craft, but go out and get another interest. I don't know—whatever you want to do: go be a dog walker, go do this, go travel.

Go have experiences because those experiences will help you in the future and will help you tell the stories that you want to tell, because you relate. I cannot stress that enough, because I spent all of my teenage years fully invested into this. Yes, I did have teenage experiences and all of that, but now more than ever, I take the time to work on other stuff in my life and to do the things that I want to do as a person, because that'll help me in the future.

Bonnie: It's sort of like getting your pond fished out. You need to restock the pond; you need to stock it with experiences that are human, that you can draw on so that you have some depth as an artist.

Victoria: Right, because if you can't relate to other people, if you can't empathize with anybody else, how are you going to have other people understand what story you are trying to tell or what song you are trying to sing or anything or what piece of art you are making? The thing about art is that you can put it out there for people to enjoy and to change people's perspectives, but if you don't have the perspective of anything else that you are trying to resonate with, then they won't really understand it.

Bonnie: You are at a great time of your life to be conscious of that. You are free to start trying all these things on. I think whether people are actors or not, that's incredibly important. It may be extra important for actors, because if you are called on to portray somebody, you want to have a clue.

Victoria: Exactly. If all you ever are is an actor—and I'm a proud actor—but if that's all you ever do, it's not going to help you. It may help you because you'll know all the technical things with your craft, but in the end, we are stepping into the lives of other people. Go out, and search for that and find that, and observe. Observing is a really big thing too.

Jessica Marie Garcia

Jessica: I think you have to feel like you're successful before you hit any dream that you want. I think it goes back to happiness. If you're not happy now, you're not going to be happy then. I wake up trying to just be so thankful and remind myself how thankful I am. My mom has been cancer-free for five years. I am so thankful for that and whenever I have a bad day, I just remember...you know what I mean?

I have an incredible fiancé who I met out here, and who I would never have met if I didn't make this plunge to come out here. I'm so thankful for the fact that *Liv and Maddie* has gone on for four years, and that I have an incredible relationship with your daughter. I got to see her grow. There are so many things to be thankful for that you have to be happy about it now. If you're not happy now, getting whatever success, you're just going to still find some problem with it.

Bonnie: I agree. People think, "After I get this, then I'll be happy." You know what? You will never get this if you're not happy first. Happiness has to come first, and it's a choice.

Jessica: It 100 percent is a choice. It's so much easier to be happy. Again, like I've told you before, I'm a dweller. I take on everyone's problems. I put them on my shoulder. I feel like I have to help everybody. I need to learn that. You know what I mean? That's an ongoing process for me that I have to just live in the moment and just let things go. I know that I don't need to fix everything, and that again comes from meditation. Success is not happiness. You have to make them two different things.

12

Advice for Young People Who Want This Life

EVERY ONE OF the actors in this book had advice for young people who want this life. And despite the fact that these twelve artists each came from different circumstances and have had very different experiences in the industry, some common themes emerged.

Making sure you love the work itself, instead of just wanting to be rich and famous, was a big theme. Staying true to yourself and taking care of yourself was another. Taking the work seriously and doing everything you can to develop your talent and always improving yourself was another common theme.

They are encouraging and also realistic, which is what you would hope for and expect from a dozen young artists who have worked hard, found success, and know directly how difficult and challenging this life can be.

Do you think you might want to be a professional actor? Read on for the advice your favorite performers have to share with you.

Booboo Stewart

Booboo: I think this world and music and entertainment, in general, it's kind of a weird thing. People say they love it, and this is their passion, but when things start going crazy and when things aren't working out for you, that's when you really find out if you love it or not. Go into it with an open mind for starters. I think working with Kenny Ortega really showed me that without telling me that.

He has the biggest mind. You know what I mean? It's so open and it's so free to suggestion, and he finds the good in everybody. For certain things, if somebody can do something, he knows what they can do and will make it work. He just has the biggest open mind.

Go into it with an open mind, and really sit down and ask yourself, "How much do I love this? Do I love this?" Because if you don't love it, it will tear you apart. It will eat you up inside, and it will be a huge battle with yourself. I think that was me and music. It was a huge battle because I got thrown into it at such an early age. I was just having fun being on tour. You know what I mean? When we were recording, I wasn't really a singer. Honestly, barely any singing lessons. I started when I got the thing. I was just dancing and having a good time. It was fantastic.

After the record deal ended, because things do end... after that ended, and after I was doing my own thing with the band and solo things with my sisters and just touring, the grind started happening. I just hit a grind, and it got really hard, and when you're playing in Six Flags for people walking by, no one cares that you're there. After going

from Staples Center to no one caring...You know what
I mean?

It's such a weird thing. I mean, sure the Staples Center
was there for you, but still when you're playing for thousands of passers-by you think, "Do I love this, or do I not
love this?" And I just did not have the love to continue
that grind. You just have to be honest with yourself
because if you don't love it, and you're getting pushed
from other people to do it, and you're doing it for other
reasons other than the fact that you really want to do it,
that's just not a healthy way to live.

Bonnie: No. It will kill your soul, I think.

Booboo: It will, and you'll end up hating it and music in general
or whatever it is. I stopped it, and I still love music. I
still play. I jam. Having that background in music to
help me with my acting and to just be a well-rounded
person and entertainer is something that I'm so proud
of and I'm so thankful that I did. I love music for that.
As a career, straight being a musician? The grind is not
for me. So really ask yourself if you love it or not. Just
be honest.

Bonnie: Your training as a triple threat is part of what's opened so
many doors for you.

Booboo: Yeah, in case the audition calls for it, like *Descendants*.
I had my song prepared going into the audition. I had a
little dance thing prepared that I was going to do in case
they asked me to dance. If I hadn't done that when I was
younger, I would have gone in there blind and just said, "I

don't really dance, and I can sing a song but..." You know what I mean?

Bonnie: And somebody else would have gotten the role.

Booboo: Exactly. Also, going into this, always know that there is someone who can do your job way better than you. Even auditioning for *Descendants*, I remember specifically sitting outside of the audition room. I could hear the guys, which is horrible, and I was listening, which is even worse. I could hear the guys singing in there, and these guys were just killing it.

I mean just singing great songs, these Disney songs. Just belting, you know, doing runs. Just amazing. I go in there; what did I sing? I sang some song from the seventies, so it's honestly the easiest song to sing. It wasn't "Rock the Boat." It was something like that.

Just the most random song. Easy chorus. I literally did the pre-chorus and the chorus, and that was it. I didn't want to do too much to where they thought, "He can't sing." I just did enough to where they knew I could hit notes, and that was it. I was out.

Bonnie: But it was good enough, obviously.

Booboo: Just always know that there's people out there that can do your job way better than you. And don't let that stop you. You've got it going. You've got to just be the best you that you can be.

Dove Cameron

Dove: Constantly keep an eye on your levels of exhaustion. I have worked myself into exhaustion before by saying yes to too much. Be honest with the people you're working with, with your family, those around you, and those who love you. Be honest with your commitments, what you can really do, what you don't think you really can, because it's a lot better for your agents, your managers, and the people who you're working for at the time to work you an hour less a day, not do that commitment on Saturday, not schedule your...whatever for really early in the morning and have you work all year than to work you really, really hard because you say you can do it and then you have to take a three- to six-month break just to recover.

This industry looks easy to some. I definitely thought it looked easy. It's not easy. It's sort of like running a marathon. You've got to start as slow as you can. People are going to want to rush you into it. You're going to want to keep an eye on your health, how you feel, what you're thinking too, because—this is huge—so many people are going to put some pretty objectifying ideas in your head.

Kids in the industry oftentimes are not raised, simply because they don't have a normal childhood; they're not raised with the same fundamental, "This is how you go from a child to an adult. This is how you maintain functionality. This is how you maintain healthy thoughts, how you don't think of yourself as a product. This is how you maintain sanity." No one is going to be pushing you to work less. No one is going to be pushing you to be more normal. It's your job and especially the parents listening to this, it is your job to save your child. It's your job to keep your kid normal, healthy, and happy. Because no one in the industry is going to be doing that for them.

Brenna D'Amico

Brenna: The littlest things you can do for yourself are never too little. Do everything and anything you can that remotely prepares you, or wiggle your way into this industry that you want to be in—taking acting classes, doing a school play, going to dance class, going to singing lessons, really anything that truly inspires you to be in this. There's nothing ever too small to prepare yourself for this crazy, beautiful business.

Bonnie: I like that, and it's really true. You did a ton of stuff before you ever came out to LA. The reason that you landed on your feet so fast in LA was because of all the work you'd done back in Chicago, back home. All those years of classes and training and practice.

Brenna: Yeah, and I think that really did help me. I think coming out here wasn't such a shock when I could see, "Oh yeah, that's kind of like back home, that's like what I've already trained for." Having that experience really did help.

Garrett Clayton

Garrett: If you think or know you want this life, especially, like I said earlier, you just have to know; in any career path you choose, there's never going to be an easy way to get whatever you want. Whether you're very successful from the beginning, the hard part is going to be learning all the ins and outs that people who've worked their way up know.

If your path is working your way up, then have patience. Remember to stay kind. Don't get jaded. Don't let other things ruin your day or ruin your life. Even for myself, I've had to remind, in any moment, if you get caught up in it for a minute and you're in the middle of shooting a movie or doing a really cool job, and you think this one dramatic thing happening at work is the be all end all, you have to have some kind of thing that helps you remember why you wanted to do it in the first place. That keeps you grounded. I have certain songs I listen to. I have people I call when I feel like I'm getting wrapped up in things that I shouldn't be. So yeah, patience, stay kind, don't worry.

People are going to say negative things and positive things about literally everything you do. You just have to trust in that, if you're doing it for the right reasons, and you're still exploring on how to grow and get better at what you do, then you'll be fine. It's just a matter of time. I had an acting coach say to me, multiple times, "Plug the pipe up with enough crap, something's bound to fall out the other end."

Bonnie: That's graphic.

Garrett: The image of it is funny, but the reality of it makes you kind of feel a little better. If you're after some kind of metaphorical dream and you're just...whether it's going to acting classes or trying to produce something or writing something and trying to get it produced, try- ing to star in something, trying to find representation or agents or managers or dance lessons, voice lessons, whatever it is, if you do enough of it long enough, you're going to learn something; you're going to progress. It's just a fact. If people see how dedicated you are, people clock that. They do not forget that in this town. If you show up, you're on time, and you care, it makes a difference, and if you have a good demeanor, that will stick with people.

People used to think movie stars can do whatever they want. Nowadays, if people hear that you're hard to work with, they will not work with you.

If you're not having fun doing what you're doing, go do something else. We don't have very much time to live our lives before we get old and we have to look back. Just enjoy your days doing what you like.

Bonnie: Yes. If you find that you change your mind or it's not what you thought it was going to be or whatever, change gears. It's okay. It's allowed. There's no shame in that. I mean, I've been a cat with several different lives, myself, and it makes life interesting. You know, you don't have to do only one thing all of your life.

Garrett: Oh yeah. It's kind of crazy. I think when people work long enough on doing one thing, that if some point, you don't really like it as much as you used to or you're not getting what you did out of it...or I guess, you're not getting the joy that you got out of it, that's okay. You're allowed to not like doing something anymore.

If you like playing video games...I guess that's an easy comparison. Your favorite video game is blah, blah, blah. You played it for years. It's usually a pretty good way just to get your mind off things, but then you want to play a different game for a while. Who cares? It's your game. It's your life. It's your time. Spend it the way you want it.

Jessica Marie Garcia

Jessica: I encourage them to think about if you would do this for free every day for the rest of your life. If you did it for free, would you do it? I think that's the most important thing because I think a lot of people think that they're going to make a bazillion dollars and they're going to be rich and famous, and that's just not what this craft is about.

If you don't think of it as a craft, if you think about it as being famous, "I want my own reality show," then go do that. Go have a reality show; go have fifteen minutes of whatever that is, but don't call yourself an actor. Call yourself a personality because I'm done with that.

To be an actor, it takes a craft, and it takes work whether that's in class or that's personal work or personal growth or whatever method, but it takes way more than just wanting your picture taken for sure. I would encourage them to learn as much as they can about it and go to school if they can afford it.

Educate yourself 110 percent on the business part of it, and just know what you're getting into. I just think it's really important that if you don't have a drama club in your school, to start a drama club, or start writing plays. I remember I even started a girl group in my chorus teacher's closet with his instruments. Anything you want to do creatively, I encourage you to do that as early as you can.

Everyone has cellphones now. Make videos. We live in a generation where it's so easy to put things up. Find little things to do that fit the craft that you want to go into. Right now, we're in a place where if you want to do animation and stuff like that, they're all available to you. You don't need a lot of money to do it. I encourage that, but learn as much as you can, and be prepared for the bumps along the road because they're going to be there.

Bonnie: Don't wait for somebody to pick you or choose you; make it happen. Be proactive.

Jessica: One hundred percent. If you think you're going to come here and someone is just going to go "I want that girl to be in my movie," that's not really how it works. It just doesn't. I think the success is in the struggle. I think the only way you're ever going to be happy with how things turn out is if you can say, "I earned this." I know that now because of what I've been through.

Joey Bragg

Joey: Take a step back. If you really think that you want to do this, think about the consequences of not doing what you want to do. Because if you really, really want to be an actor and you are the best in your school and you're attractive enough to be a leading lady, think about the consequences of going to a place away from your family and throwing yourself at a wall and hoping that somebody grabs you before you fall. It's not in your favor to make it in this business, so you really have to be okay with not making it if you want to make it.

You have to wholeheartedly understand that you could spend the next ten years of your life scared and homeless, and you have to be okay with the consequences because there are so many kids that think, "Oh, it takes a long time, takes a couple years, and then you get a job," but it's not. It doesn't. There are certain people that come here. In the first three months, they get a job, and there are people that have been here for years and years and years and haven't gotten a job, and it's not talent. A lot of people say it's talent. It's not talent. It's the right person to see you. It's how you look. A lot of people think it's looks. It's not. It's just random. It's just absolutely random.

You have to be 100 percent okay with not being what you want because there's so many people that come here and want to be an actor and then aren't an actor and get upset, but you knew that was a possibility. Coming here and knowing that it probably won't happen is the mindset that I think everybody needs to have.

You can go to acting class every day and be the best actor in the world and never work. As long as you are satisfied or happy with going to an acting class and that being the acting, then that's fine.

Be okay with busking. That's going to be my memoir. Be okay with going out there and doing and being a street performer and making that kind of money before you think that going to LA is going to be a magical red carpet ride to stardom because it's not.

Cameron Boyce

Cameron: I think everybody would say that you really just have to make sure that you are actually passionate about it, and for the right reasons. If you're passionate about becoming famous, that's not a good deal. First of all, you're probably not going to be famous, if that's all you want. And second of all, if you do become famous, you're going to become one of those people, right? We all know who those people are.

Bonnie: Famous for the wrong reasons.

Cameron: Right, exactly. So honestly, just make sure that you are passionate about the craft, about actually working hard and everything that comes with it—and there are a lot of things that come with it, just make sure that you're cool with all that. I've been in it for a long time, more than half my life, and I'm eighteen, which is so crazy. But just stay persistent, because it doesn't come overnight.

And make sure that you are at least trying new things, improving. Make sure that you're not doing the same things over and over again. It's very easy to get sides and an audition and whatever and just sort of fall into a method or a certain way of doing things. Treat a script the way it should be treated. Every script is different. Every character is different. Don't play it the same way that you played your audition two days ago, you know? Really just give the script the respect that it deserves, right?

And yeah, if you don't book something in six months, if you don't book something in a year, if you don't book something in three years, just remember that you have a passion for it and that's why you do it, and not for any other reason. Do it for yourself. Don't do it for somebody telling you that it's a good idea or…I see a lot of actors who get into it because acting seems easy. Acting seems like a good deal. Like, you go on set and you say a couple lines.

It is not easy. There's nothing about it that's easy. And so much of that is because there are so many things that are unknown, so many things that you can't control. Performers are passionate about this. We drive ourselves crazy. Talking about an audition after an audition…you will never see a person more passionate. And honestly, for me, I just try to forget because there are so many things that you wanted to convey and wanted to show that you didn't get a chance to in the audition, and you'll just pull your hair out. But that's all a part of the process. And when you are right for a character and right for a role, it'll happen. The stars will align, and you will be able to do it. And that's what you always have to fall back on. When the character's right, when the time is right, when everything lines up, it will work.

I like to think, not that I'm really an "Everything happens for a reason" kind of guy, but at the same time, it kind of does. That's sort of what it is. If you're not supposed to play a character, you're not going to play that character. And even if you really love the character…I'd much rather hear, "You're not right for this" than to be cast and still not be right for it and do a bad job.

That's the worst possible scenario. So just trust the process. And trust other people's opinions about you.

They're going to say, "Hey, you were great, but this is not right. This is not your role." And in that scenario, let it go. Let it be.

Whatever it is that you're doing in life, just make sure that you're staying true to yourself. That's the most important thing. And actors have a hard time with that because we play characters and we're different people for half of the year. We do a lot of different things and have a lot of people pulling us a lot of different ways, and I'm so glad that I've been able to find this within myself. But if I feel that something is happening in my career where I'm not being myself, I shut it down, which is very important. And even if it will get more followers, more famous, a better role, a better this, a better that, I don't care. I'm going to be myself because frankly, that's all that I've got. And when you lose yourself, you lose everything. So just be yourself. And that's it.

Thomas Doherty

Thomas: People can only speak from their own experience, and everyone's experience is different. So everyone's advice is going to be different. That can get really, really confusing. Life's one of those things where it teaches you as you live it, you know? I think if you have fundamental principles, kindness, compassion, and also a drive, not just exclusively for a career, but a drive to understand yourself—understand the workings of your mind and the workings of your body—but it's one of those things; life just teaches you how to live it. I think if you just focus on being a kind, compassionate person, empathetic, understanding, and just look for the joy in life, gradually you'll just stumble upon things.

I think that's the thing; you need to do the stumbling first, like going to an audition for the first time. You're going to be anxious, nervous, sweat, feel sick, maybe cry. But it's one of those things you've got to do; you've got to stumble until you can walk.

Bonnie: It's good life advice.

Thomas: It's kind of annoying advice, but you know...acceptance then; just accept. Because the more you accept the inevitable, the more you can make peace with that, and then you can progress.

Luke Benward

Luke: If you really, really want to do it, go for it. Unless it's a weird situation like mine, and it just kind of happens to fall into place. Start locally and see if you really actually enjoy acting. That's what's going to keep you happy. If you enjoy what you're doing and what you're bringing to the table, and you are just confident, then that's where you're going to find your joy and your passion moving forward. If you just want to be in magazines and famous, it's very cliché to say, but it's just going to be sad. It's just a recipe for disaster.

Yeah, if you don't enjoy being on stage—I'm not going to say auditioning—but being on stage or being in front of a camera, the actual performance, when you're on—and you have to nail it—if you don't love doing that, then find something else because there's way too many people trying to do it that don't love it, and they're obviously taking roles from actors who do love it, as much as I hate to say it, but they are.

Figure it out. Because fame is fleeting. Everyone knows that. Fame is here and gone. It can destroy lives. It's not anything to mess around with. That's really my advice. Figure out if you love it, and if you love it, go for it. If not, you can find something you do love.

Sarah Jeffery

Sarah: I would definitely like to remind you it's possible. It's not impossible. It takes a lot of work and dedication. You might need help from your parents. It is helpful to know people; I won't lie. It's helpful to get advice. This book is going to be incredible. This podcast is going to be so helpful.

Do what you can. Work hard; take classes; research, whether that's looking at people in everyday life, whether it's watching movies, reading books. Do what you can to build on your knowledge. If it's something you really want, and it's meant to happen for you, it absolutely will. It's easy to get caught up in the idea of it and not the actual craft.

I think it's easy to look at people's Instagram pages and be like, "Wow, you are doing all these cool photo shoots and you have all these cool products being sent to you." It is not about that. When it comes down to it, it's the work, the long hours, being exhausted when you get home and having to get up the next day. As long as you keep in mind that it's actually work, it's not all fun and games…it is fun. Love your craft, and it'll be good.

Victoria Moroles

Victoria: At least for me, I feel like what I would tell myself when I was first starting out is to just have fun. If you do want to do this and you take an interest in it, and you feel like you have a passion behind it, then always stay focused on that feeling. So many other things are going to come up. There are going to be so many blockers from that feeling, that passionate feeling that you feel when you first want to start, and you first want to really do this.

There are going to be piles of things that are just coming at you and getting on top of that feeling and really weighing on that feeling. You've just got to stay in tune with that and always have that feeling at the base of whatever you are doing. Whether it be auditioning or working or going to class or working on something in your bedroom, to just stay present within that and be patient. I know I already talked about it, but be patient, and persevere, and stay strong, and just have fun.

If you are not feeling it, one day, you are not having fun, don't do it anymore. If I'm ever not having fun, ever, I'm not going to do it anymore.

If you like art, and you want to be an artist, then dabble in other things. Open your creative mind, and really get out there and figure out everything that you could do, because it's only going to help you as an actor.

I would definitely say to keep experiencing life the way you would, maybe not exactly the way you would if you weren't an actor, but definitely keep experiencing and doing things, and don't make it your complete life.

I love thinking about when I first started, when I first wanted to do this. Just hold onto that feeling. It made me so happy coming to talk with you because it reminded me of that feeling. You really do get away from that. It's always there, but there are so many things that come in front of it.

Just come back to that passionate drive that you have, and let those little blockers come in the way, kind of push them out of the way, and then just keep proceeding.

Dylan Playfair

Dylan: I would say, "Do it. In any capacity that you can. That, I think, will really shed light onto whether or not you want to make it your everything." For me, it was a little taste of being on stage in high school. That, coupled with the feeling I got when I told stories around friends. If you know deep in your heart that that's what makes you happy, do it.

There's some motivational speaker named Les Brown, and he says, "The wealthiest place in the world is the graveyard." In the graveyard is where every single unfulfilled dream and idea ends up. If you've got a passion or an idea or something that you know you could put your energy behind, you owe it to yourself and the world... what if you create something that changes the world? If you never pursue that, that dies with you. That's really sad. I think people kill that off in themselves way too often. Don't let the special things die with you. If you know they exist, give them life. Only you can give them life, whatever that may be. If you want to be a painter, a doctor, if you want to be the best lawyer in the world, give those dreams the ability to live.

Enjoy what you do. Love what you do, and you'll never work. That's it.

Epilogue

I want to leave you with some final thoughts from a few of the young actors who so generously shared their experience with you in this book.

Garrett Clayton hopes you remember, "Luck is preparation meets opportunity.' That's ninety-nine percent of my life."

Thomas Doherty emphasizes that joy can't be found outside of yourself, in the trappings of fame and material success. "You can only find that joy inside of you."

And Dove Cameron wishes you luck, and says, "I actually hope that you join me because it's incredible over here."

I wish you luck too.

Read on for some final words of wisdom and encouragement.

Garrett Clayton

Garrett: I just don't want everyone to take away that my ser-
              endipitous moments were just by chance. I was always
              seeking out the opportunities that I found. When I got
              the *Days of Our Lives* casting call, that prompted me to
              find the roommates that I mentioned earlier; that was
              because I went to the casting call that had fifteen hun-
              dred people. When I found that manager, it was because I
              drove three hours while I was doing *High School Musical 2*
              on stage.

              My friend Emily and I knew we had a show that night,
              and the casting call was three hours away, so we woke
              up extra early that day, drove three hours...and both
              of these casting calls had fifteen hundred people,
              because they love to tell you how many people are in
              line at these casting calls. All of these serendipitous
              moments were found, and they happened because I
              sought out the opportunity. I worked for it, and I found
              a way to make it work. That's, I think, the biggest thing
              I hope people take away, that nothing was ever handed;
              it was always sought out. I always looked for the oppor-
              tunities. That's nine times out of ten, all people need
              to do.

Bonnie: I agree. What is that saying...Luck favors the prepared?

Garrett: Luck is preparation meets opportunity. That's 99 percent
              of my life.

              Any good opportunity I've had, it's because I'm always
              studying. I'm always going to voice lessons, dance classes,

acting coaching, and workshops. Anything I can get my hands on, I want to try, I want to do, I want to work on it. The same acting coach who said the pipe thing told me, "This right here, this is your instrument. If you're a musician, this is what you play." She goes, "So you need to know every facet of it."

Bonnie: From your foot to your head, for those of you who can't see what he's doing.

Garrett: Yeah. So I'm pointing to my foot and my head. We talked about exploring your past and experiences you've had to feeling comfortable with your body because you can embody the character in your mind, but how does that character physically move? That's what your mind and your body is...it's an instrument.

Thomas Doherty

Thomas: You've just got to find joy in your life. I can't emphasize more that you can't find joy outside of you. You can find pleasure outside of you, but pleasure again is like the sugar analogy: it's a quick fix. You can only find that joy inside of you.

The more you understand yourself, the more you familiarize you with yourself; surely, that's going to be amazing for acting, because you understand yourself. You understand how to manipulate yourself into being someone else. So I think the root is honestly, before you even think about acting, to get a fundamental grasp of you, of who you are. What I mean is if you can understand yourself, then everything will fall into place.

Dove Cameron

Dove: I want you to know...everything that I shared today was as truthful as I could possibly be, and some of that stuff is maybe nicer than you've heard, because some people will try to scare you. You know, that's my real experience. Everything that I shared has been my authentic experience, and some of the stuff was probably harsher than you've heard, but I would never want to waste an opportunity to speak unedited to parents who are interested with their kid getting into this or kids who are listening to this.

Bonnie: A lot of high school and college students actually listen to the podcast.

Dove: Well, for anybody who's interested, I hope that you gleaned something from my thoughts today, and I do not in any way intend to scare you away from this industry. I actually hope that you join me because it's incredible over here. Like I said—if you take care of yourself.

I hope you figure it out. I hope somebody gives you that chance. I think if you're really looking into it as hard as you must be to be listening to podcasts, reading books, and doing the research, I respect the living daylights out of you because that is part of it. Good on you for doing your due diligence, and I wish you luck, and I hope to work with you one day. I send you good vibes. Good luck. Love you, guys.

Did you love this book? Do you want *more*?

Go to https://bonniejwallace.com/bonus-chapters/ to download *free bonus chapters* that weren't included in the final manuscript due to length issues. Find out what it was like for these young actors to land in Hollywood, who inspires them, what they would do if they weren't actors, how they stay focused on their dreams, and *more*!

Mini Bios of Actors

Luke Benward

Luke began his professional acting career at the age of five playing Mel Gibson's son in *We Were Soldiers*. He then went on to star in many TV shows and films, including *How to Eat Fried Worms, Because of Winn-Dixie, Cloud 9, Dumplin', Life of the Party, Good Luck Charlie, Ravenswood, The Goldbergs,* and more.

Cameron Boyce

Cameron has been acting professionally since he was eight. He is best known for his roles on *Mirrors, Grown Ups, Grown Ups 2, Jake and the Neverland Pirates, Jessie, Gamer's Guide to Pretty Much Everything, Descendants, Descendants 2, and Descendants 3.*

Joey Bragg

Joey began his career in stand-up comedy at the age of thirteen, performing in clubs throughout the San Francisco Bay area. His film and TV credits include *Liv and Maddie, Father of the Year, The Outfield, Reach, Mark & Russell's Wild Ride, Wet Hot American Summer: 10 Years Later,* and more.

Dove Cameron

Dove was cast in her first professional role at fifteen. She is best known for *Liv and Maddie, Descendants, Descendants 2, Descendants 3, Agents of Shield, Hairspray Live, Dumplin', Barely Lethal, Cloud 9, Marvel Rising: Secret Warriors, Angry Birds 2, The Mentalist, and more.* She won an Emmy for her work on *Liv and Maddie,* is a Columbia Records artist, and is originating the role of Cher in *Clueless, the Musical.*

Garrett Clayton

Garrett arrived in Hollywood at the age of nineteen and landed his first role on *Days of Our Lives.* Since then his many film and TV credits include *Teen Beach Movie, Teen Beach 2, Hairspray Live, The Real O'Neills, The Fosters, King Cobra, Don't Hang Up, The Last Breakfast Club, Reach,* and *Between Worlds.*

Brenna D'Amico

Brenna was cast in her first professional role in *Descendants* when she was fifteen. Her film and TV credits also include *Descendants 2, Descendants 3, Descendants: Wicked World, The Middle, Keys, Overnights, Chicken Girls, Code Black,* and *The Relic.*

Thomas Doherty

Thomas trained at the MGA Academy of Performing Arts in Edinburgh, Scotland, before landing his first professional role in *The Lodge* at twenty-one. His other film and TV credits include *Descendants 2, Descendants 3, High Strung: Free Dance, The Two Wolves,* and *Catherine the Great.*

Jessica Marie Garcia

Jessica arrived in Hollywood at the age of eighteen and landed her first role on *Huge.* Her TV and film projects since include *The Middle, Liv and Maddie, Betch, How to Get Away with Murder,*

Starter Pack, and *Avenge the Crows.* She is currently filming season two of the acclaimed Netflix series *On My Block.*

Sarah Jeffery
Sarah's first break came through a voice-over role at fourteen for Cartoon Network. She is best known for film and TV roles on *Rogue, Wayward Pines, Descendants, Descendants 3, The X-Files, Shades of Blue, Daphne & Velma,* and *Charmed.*

Victoria Moroles
Victoria moved to Los Angeles when she was twelve and got her first role on *CSI: Crime Scene Investigation.* TV and film projects that followed have included *Cloud 9, Legends, Teen Wolf, Liv and Maddie, Here and Now,* and *Down a Dark Hall.*

Dylan Playfair
Dylan began his career in film and TV at the age of nineteen, and the many TV and film projects since have included *Some Assembly Required, Haters Back Off, Descendants 2, Descendants 3, Travelers, Letterkenny, If I Had Wings, The Drop,* and *The Order.*

Booboo Stewart
Booboo began his career in film and TV at the age of ten doing stunt work, and his big break came playing Seth Clearwater in the *Twilight Saga: Breaking Dawn* and *Twilight Saga: Eclipse.* Of his many roles since, he is best known for *Descendants, Descendants 2, Descendants 3, X-Men: Days of Future Past,* and *Marvel Rising: Secret Warriors.*

Social Media Links (All verified accounts)

Luke Benward
Twitter: @lukebenward
Instagram: @labenward

Cameron Boyce
Twitter: @TheCameronBoyce
Instagram: @TheCameronBoyce

Joey Bragg
Twitter: @joeybragg
Instagram: @joeybragg
Facebook: @joeybraggcomedy

Dove Cameron
Twitter: @DoveCameron
Instagram: @DoveCameron
Facebook: @OfficialDoveCameron

Garrett Clayton
Twitter: @garrettclayton1
Instagram: @garrettclayton1
Facebook: @GarrettClaytonLove

Brenna D'Amico
Twitter: @brennadamico
Instagram: @brennadamico
Facebook: @officialbrennadamico

Thomas Doherty
Twitter: @thomasadoherty
Instagram: @thomasadoherty

Jessica Marie Garcia
Twitter: @JessMarieGarcia
Instagram: @jess_m_garcia

Sarah Jeffery
Twitter: @sarahmjeffery3
Instagram: @sarahmjeffery
Facebook: OfficialSarahJeffery

Victoria Moroles
Twitter: @victoriamoroles
Instagram: @victoriamoroles
Facebook: @victoriamoroles

Dylan Playfair
Twitter: @DylanPlayfair
Instagram: @DylanPlayfair1

Booboo Stewart
Instagram: @BoobooStewart.Art
Twitter: @BoobooStewart

About the Author

Bonnie J. Wallace is the author of the acclaimed *Hollywood Parents Guide* and producer of the popular *Hometown to Hollywood* podcast, and writes a blog for parents of young actors at bonniejwallace.com as well as regular articles for Backstage.com as a Backstage Expert. She teaches and speaks on the acting business for parents at panels and events across the country.

Bonnie also offers private consultations with parents who want to help their child become a happy professional actor, because every family's path is unique.

Mother of Dove Cameron, an Emmy Award–winning actress and Columbia Records artist, star of *Liv and Maddie, Disney Descendants, Hairspray Live, Agents of Shield, Dumplin', Clueless, the Musical,* and more, Bonnie is dedicated to educating and inspiring others on this journey. Find out more at www.bonniejwallace.com.

Follow Bonnie here:
Website: www.bonniejwallace.com
Twitter: @bonniejwallace
Instagram: @bonniejwallace
Facebook: @BonnieJWallaceConsulting

Made in the USA
Columbia, SC
07 May 2019